Sin City Greed

James C. Molet

Also By James C. Molet

Fiction
Cream City Hustle

Non-Fiction
Rendezvous With Retirement: A Guide to Getting Fiscally Fit

Published by JCM Publishing, Sierra Vista, AZ 85635.

ISBN: 978-0-9895505-6-7

Sin City Greed

Subscribe to http://RetirementSavvy.net, where personal finance, with a focus on retirement planning, is covered via Discussions, Recommendations, Interviews, Quizzes and the Living Frugally series.

CONTENTS

ACKNOWLEDGMENTS

My sincere gratitude and appreciation are extended to the following who helped to bring this second novel into being:

My wife, Karen, my daily sounding board, my biggest cheerleader and the partner that makes most of my successes possible.

My brother, Kem, and our parents, John and Loretta. Their support and encouragement was instrumental in bringing my first novel, *Cream City Hustle*, into existence, and has continued with this effort. In addition to their encouragement they served as informal reviewers, adding their insights and critiques, each step of the way as the story progressed.

Thank you all.

PROLOGUE

Las Vegas. Near the intersection of Paradise and East Flamingo Roads. From his second story office Carlton F. Morrison III, the founder and CEO of Blackstone Financial Services Group, watched as the sun set on the mid-June day. Soon the distant lights would shine bright and the world famous strip would come to life.

"Do you require anything else this evening, Mr. Morrison?" Darlene, his administrative assistant, asked as she rapped lightly on his open door and peeked through the doorway.

"No, Dear, nothing else tonight. I just need to tie up a few loose ends and then I will be out of here. Have a good night."

"Thank you. You too, Mr. Morrison."

He'd made the decision a few days ago but had put off actually doing it. Now there was no time. He had received the second notification from Bank of Las Vegas earlier today. If he didn't get a significant infusion of capital soon, the boutique investment advisory firm he had spent 17 years building from nothing would wither and die here in the Nevada desert. He required additional capital and they required proof of liquid assets before they would increase his credit limit. He had three days.

"How did it come to this?" Carl asked the empty room. Predictably, no answer was forthcoming. It seemed like a lifetime ago that BFSG was humming right along. Both Divisions, Equities – where most of his client's money was invested – and Real Estate – where most of the firm's money was invested to fund internal operations - were performing spectacularly. That was no longer the case. While the Equities Division continued to post strong returns, the Real Estate Division had been devastated over the last few years as he had increased his real estate holdings, a mistake in hindsight, just as the meltdown in the Las Vegas housing market accelerated.

He had three days to increase the balance in his Bank of the West account and submit a statement to Bank of Las Vegas. He only had one source of capital at his disposal ... client accounts from the Equities Division. Sitting down at his desk, he woke his computer from sleep mode and opened the BFSG Client's Accounts spreadsheet, the document containing all relevant data, including account holdings and balances. The first order of business? Copying the document, creating a shadow spreadsheet.

With the two spreadsheets open on his dual monitor setup, he pulled up the first client account, Jim and Phyllis Abbott, and placed their upcoming quarterly statement on the desktop with the original spreadsheet. With an account balance of $1,784,200.61 at the end of the previous month, they were among his more affluent clients. Next, he opened Photoshop, where it shared the second monitor with the shadow spreadsheet. Seven minutes later he had removed $75,000 from the Abbott's account and deposited the money into BFSG's corporate account with Bank of the West. The Abbott's quarterly statement - the one scheduled to be mailed next Tuesday - was 'updated' to show a new balance of $1,892,935.93. That was just about in line with the 6% monthly return he guaranteed his clients.

Next up was Charles Bingman with an account balance of $1,082,369.29. "You've done pretty well for yourself at only 58, Charles," Carl mumbled into the dimly lit room. Forty eight clients later, the Bank of the West account showed an updated balance of $3,831,527.03. A significant difference from the starting balance of $81,527.03. Glancing at the clock, he saw that it was 1:26 a.m. God it was late. He needed to get home. He was absolutely drained. Saving all of his documents, with the shadow documents saved to an external hard drive, he placed his computer in sleep mode and made his way to the kitchenette area. With the external hard drive safely ensconced in the wall safe, he turned off the lights and locked the office door behind him.

Somewhere deep inside, Carl knew this was the beginning of the end.

[1] RETIREMENT

HENDERSON, NEVADA – 15 MONTHS LATER

Located at the southern edge of the Las Vegas Valley, Sun City Anthem in Henderson, Nevada is perched in the foothills of the Black Mountains 800 feet above the valley floor. Only twenty-five minutes from the Las Vegas strip, this active adult community couldn't be more different from its world famous neighbor to the north. Here the hustle and bustle; and the glitz of the city was replaced with active, though more reserved, retirement living.

The glossy, bright colored brochures advertised that 'Life in Sun City Anthem is filled with a never-ending array of fun activities, club meetings, classes and fun events. In addition to the three clubhouses and two 18-hole golf courses, there are over 50 clubs and interest groups that include everything from sports and fitness to arts and crafts. Other exciting clubs include ballroom dance, bocce ball, ceramics, bridge, performing arts, music groups and much more.'

Vallory, a retired orthodontist, was among those for whom the golf courses were a key reason they were drawn to this oasis in the desert. Most visitors to Vegas have no idea this slice of heaven is home to one of the premiere golf clubs in Southern Nevada, the Revere Golf Club. The residents, those who golf anyway, lauded it for the challenges it presented and its pristine beauty. Perfectly merged with the rugged desert valleys and canyons of the foothills, both Revere Golf Club courses offered spectacular views of the Las Vegas Strip to the north and the surrounding mountain ranges.

This morning, while many of Vegas' visitors - and a smaller number of its residents - were dealing with hangovers and bemoaning last night's losses on the blackjack or craps tables; recounting their Cirque du Soleil experience or debating which was better, the Blue Man Group or Penn & teller, Vallory and Sandra were playing the Lexington Course, the 7,143-yard, par-72 course that Vallory preferred to the 7,034-yard Concord Course favored by Sandra.

"Next week we're playing the Concord," Sandra emphatically informed Vallory as she straightened up from teeing up her ball.

"That's fine with me. I can be just as bad over there. My badness knows no bounds."

"Just as long we continue to enjoy ourselves. Above all else, we strive for self pleasure," said Sandra.

"What was that?" asked Vallory, giving her friend a wink and a nod.

"Girl, you know what I mean. Get your mind out of the gutter." The friends laughed as Vallory took a couple more practice swings. Planting her feet and flexing her knees, she maintained eye contact with the ball as she started her backswing.

"Fore!" Vallory and Sandra yelled out in perfect harmony as Vallory's tee shot started off slightly to the right and hooked severely back to its left and zeroed in on the golfers on the 7th fairway.

"Last Thursday I was giving it my best Benihana imitation, slicing it all over the place, now I'm hooking it every other tee shot. Oh the misery. This game is killing me!"

"Practice, practice, practice," Sandra encouraged her friend as she teed up her own ball.

"What do you think about those new Nike balls?" Vallory asked. "I'm thinking about trying some new ones."

"Girl, I have no idea," responded Sandra. "I'm playing Titleist balls; have been for the last two years. However, it does seem to me that the Nikes aren't doing much for Tiger lately."

"Ouch! That's just mean. Just plain old mean. True, but mean."

"What's George doing this morning?" Vallory inquired.

"Swimming ... " Sandra began.

"He's not wearing Speedos is he?" Vallory asked. "Nobody outside of Olympians should ever wear those things."

"No," Sandra assured her. "I love my man, but that's an image I'm trying to strike from my own mind." After they had a good laugh, Sandra continued, "you know my husband, if he can't get a tee time earlier than 8:00 a.m. during the summer he doesn't want to play. If I do manage to drag him out to the course after 8:00 all he does is bitch. The last thing I want to hear is him bitching. He wanted to check out the indoor pool over at the new clubhouse so I told him to go ahead."

"That's the solar powered one, right?"

"That's right. I haven't been over there yet but it's supposed to have an indoor pool, an outdoor pool, tennis courts, pickle ball courts and bocce ball courts."

"Sounds good. We'll have to check it out soon. Don't expect me to play that bocce ball though."

"Why not?"

"I can't stand that game. Plus, it sounds like an Italian venereal disease to me." Sandra had to regroup after a good laugh to prepare for her tee shot. "Where do you come up with that stuff? You kill me. You really do absolutely kill me."

Her final practice swing out of the way, Sandra steadied her feet, took one last look down the fairway and released her tee shot. Straight down the middle of the fairway.

"Nice drive, Sandra," said Vallory as they celebrated with a solid fist bump before jumping in the cart.

"Well let's go find your ball, Ms. Jackson. Oh, and remind me to text George when we get to the 17th. He should be finished lap swimming well before we're finished here and he wants to meet us at Buckman's Grille. He absolutely loves the lunch menu over there."

"That sounds good. I'll be ready for a club sandwich and a beer myself by the time we're finished. I'll make sure it's a light beer though. I need to maintain my girlish figure," Vallory joked.

"You and me both, sister. You and me both," said Sandra. "I think I'll have some of that prickly pear lemonade instead of a beer."

Finding her ball, Vallory quickly punched it to the middle of the fairway, 15 yards in front of Sandra's ball.

"Did you hear about Janice?" Sandra asked.

"Smith or Walker?"

"Walker. That's the one that lives over on Evergreen Oaks Drive, right?"

"Yep, Vallory affirmed."What's going on with her?"

"Hold on. Let me put this 6-iron to work first."

"Nice shot, Sandra. You should be able to chip on from there." Using a 7-iron as her weapon of choice, Vallory's third shot landed on the front edge of the green.

"Nice shot, Ms. Jackson." A chip and a putt later, Sandra finished off the 14th hole, as did Vallory two putts later.

"So what happened to Janice?" Vallory inquired.

"Well you know her husband, Bill's his name I think, got laid off from his job last year."

"Yep, Bill is his name and yes I did hear."

"Well apparently she lost that part-time job she had."

"So what's the deal? Are they hurting for money now or something?"

"Apparently they were getting by, but just barely, after Bill lost his job last year. I heard they needed her job and the extra money because they're still carrying a mortgage on their house."

"What!?" Vallory said incredulously. "At their ages? They've got to be 70 if not older. What the hell were they thinking?"

"Hold on. We've got a couple of roadrunners behind us."

"Let's just wave them through," suggested Vallory.

"Good idea."

As the pair that was behind them moved on through, Sandra noted that according to Mary Presser, one of the members of their little group of eight, Janice's husband wanted to keep their money in their investment accounts and not use the money to pay off the mortgage.

"I guess that can make sense if you're younger and the rate of return on your investments is greater than the interest rate on your mortgage. But damn, when you get to be our age … "

"Or anywhere near our age," Sandra suggested.

"When you get to be our age it makes more sense to just pay off your mortgage. Without a mortgage your expenses are lower, which means you'll need less income when you're retired," suggested Vallory.

"Especially when you're older and may not be able to work, or like them, you lose your jobs. Hell, George wouldn't let us go into retirement with a mortgage. He insisted that we go into retirement without a mortgage. In fact, he insisted on no debt at all. No mortgage, auto loan or credit card debt."

"Absolutely," Vallory said, "I read some article online recently that said nearly one in three Americans at least 60 years old has debt, and the average balance of that debt is more than $60,000."

"To have that kind of debt at 60 is crazy, particularly if you are thinking about retiring."

"Yep, if that's the situation you're in, paying off that debt should be the thing on your mind, not retirement."

Working their way through the 15th and 16th holes, Vallory playing them at a +1 and Sandra a +2, Sandra pulled out her phone and sent her husband a text: *to George - Teeing off at the 17th*. Matching each other shot for shot, the friends managed pars on the par 4 hole. No such luck on the 18th. Standing over her teed ball and halfway through her backswing, Sandra was distracted by a bee and hooked the ball left.

"Shucky darn! I should have backed off the second I sensed that bee instead of trying to swing through." Watching her friend's tee shot, and determined not to hook it on the last hole, Vallory stepped confidently to the tee ... and proceeded to do exactly that. The shot would have been perfect on a dog leg left. Unfortunately, the fairway was straight as an arrow.

"I'll be damned!" Vallory cried out, "after avoiding that shot the last couple of holes, try as I might I couldn't avoid it on the last hole."

"Well, at least it looks like they landed in the same area." Jumping in their cart they headed down the left side of the fairway in search of their balls. No luck. After six minutes of searching they called it a day.

"Well I don't know about you," Vallory said, "but I'm hot as hell and I'm tired of looking for that damn ball."

"You and me both, Val. Forget those balls and let's get out of here. The sun is getting a little too high in the sky to still be messin' around out here. George should be there by now anyway."

"Yep. I'm ready for a cold beer and something to eat," declared Vallory.

Making their way to Buckman's Grille, voted 'the best 19th hole' by *Vegas Golf Digest* magazine the last two years, Vallory asked Sandra what she thought they should do for their birthday's this year. Scorpios both, they often celebrated their birthdays together in the merry, merry month of November. Last year, the big 60 for Vallory, she had the honor of selecting the celebratory activity; a group cruise to Belize. Turning 60 this year, it was Sandra's turn.

"I haven't even thought about it yet to tell you the truth. One thing I do know is that I don't want any kind of surprise like we pulled on George three years ago. I'd die of a damn heart attack. I don't know, we'll come up with something, amiga."

"Sounds good."

Removing her sunglasses and looking past the hostess in the lobby, Sandra didn't see her husband after the first scan of the dining area.

"There he is," Vallory said, tapping her on the shoulder. George and Charles Bingman, one of the members of their group of eight had grabbed a booth.

"What took you ladies so long?" asked Charles, as Vallory and Sandra approached the booth. "Hope you don't mind, but we started on the libations without you," he noted as he raised his beer in a solo toast. Sliding into the booth next to George and Charles, Sandra and Vallory ordered draft beers when the waiter approached.

"Hold on," said Sandra as she waved toward the door. "I just saw some friends walk in. Can we get a larger table?"

"Absolutely," said the young waiter. "Give me just a minute and I'll slide a couple tables together."

"Thank you."

"I thought you were going to get a prickly pear lemonade?" said Vallory.

"I changed my mind. A cold beer sounds good; that should hit the spot. It was warm out there this morning."

Two minutes later, Dave and Mary Presser, at 56 each, the youngest among their group of friends, joined them as the group relocated to the larger table.

"It looks like we almost have the entire group here," said Dave as he and his wife sat down.

"Everybody except Bill and Chad," noted George.

"How is Chad's mom doing anyway?" asked Mary.

"Not too bad apparently," Vallory said, "I got an email from him yesterday. He said she finished her last round of chemotherapy this week and so far, things look good. I guess he'll have to wait and see. He said he's still trying to convince her to move out here with him and Bill but she refuses. She wants to stay there in Tampa. She sounds ornery as hell."

"Quite frankly, I don't know how anybody could live there with all that damn humidity," said Charles, shaking his head side to side.

"I'm with you, Charles," Sandra said, "I absolutely prefer the dry heat. The combination of heat and moisture is just way too uncomfortable."

"Too many damn mosquitoes for me. I'm starting to itch just thinking about it," said Vallory as she reached across with her left hand and scratched her right shoulder.

"Stop, now you've got me scratching," Mary protested as they all got in a good laugh.

"Anyway," Vallory said, "they're supposed to be back tomorrow. We'll have to all get together. Maybe a little cookout or something on Saturday. I volunteer Dave and Mary. All in favor say aye."

"Aye," the four friends quickly responded in unison.

"I guess we'll host a little cookout," said Mary, turning to her husband.

"It looks that way," responded Dave. "How does grilled bologna sound? You know we're working on a tight budget," he said, laughing.

"You sound just like my nephew, Train," said Vallory. "He's always going on about not having any money and being on a tight budget. Steaks or bologna don't make a difference to me. Either is fine. Regardless, we're not letting you two off the hook. Whatever you're serving, we're eating." The group nodded their heads in agreement.

"So how was your round?" asked Mary, glancing first at Sandra and then Vallory. "Which course did you play?"

"We played the Lexington," said Sandra. I prefer the Concord, but it wasn't too bad."

"Yeah. Other than slicing the ball all over the place and both of us losing our balls on the 18th, it was a great round," noted Vallory with a hint of sarcasm. "Next week we move our game over to the Concord."

"Should be interesting," said Sandra.

"Did you play this morning, George?" asked Mary.

"Nope. They went too late for me; it's a little too hot. I went and swam at the new clubhouse."

"How was it?" asked Charles.

"It was good. It is a beautiful facility. They really did a nice job. I swam for about 45 minutes; a good workout. It felt good to get back in the pool. It's probably been two or three months since I swam last."

"We'll have to go check it out," said Dave, glancing at his wife. "Maybe play a little bocce ball."

"Don't say it, Val," said Sandra, looking over at her friend.

"What's that?" asked Mary.

"You know how Val's mind works. She has some interesting thoughts on bocce ball ... you don't want to know."

"Tampa International Airport must have the worst layout in the world. I hate this place. It's worse than McCarran. Which terminal are we looking for again?"

"For the third time, Chad, Southwest is in the Airside C terminal. Where did you put the boarding passes?"

"Excuse me?"

"The boarding passes. Where did you put the boarding passes?"

"Shoot! I knew I forgot something this morning. I forgot to print them out at my mom's house. We'll have to stop at the ticket counter to get our boarding passes and drop off the bags."

"Oh well, it is what it is. Please don't be too crowded," Bill pleaded to the airline Gods.

"At the counter or at the TSA checkpoint," Chad added. "We're getting close on time, about 35 minutes before they're scheduled to start boarding."

"We'll be okay, Babe," Bill assured him. "Let's just get to that ticket counter quickly." After waiting in line anxiously for five or six minutes, getting their boarding passes, checking their bags and making their way through security, Chad and Bill made it to their gate with seven minutes to spare.

"It will be good to get home and out of this incessant heat and humidity," said Chad as he plopped down in the worn, tired looking chair in the gate area.

"I'm just glad your mom is doing better. I do wish she would consider moving to Nevada and staying near us. It would be so much easier on everybody," Bill suggested.

"It would," Chad agreed, "but unfortunately, she is not hearing that at all right now. That old bird is fiercely independent. That's part of why I love her so much. Do you see any of those charging stations nearby? I need to charge this damn phone."

Conducing a quick 360 degree scan of the area, Bill noted, "there are a couple over there, just behind that young couple."

"Hold on a sec, it looks like that gate agent is getting ready to make an announcement :

> "Ladies and gentlemen, our aircraft has arrived at the gate. We will start boarding Southwest flight 558 with non-stop service to Las Vegas in about five minutes. Group A, positions 1 - 30, may start lining up to my left; positions 31 - 60 may start lining up on the right. We will call for Group B when we have finished boarding Group A, positions 1 - 30. Thank you for your patience."

"Which group are we in?" Bill inquired.

"It will be a few minutes, we're B 52 and 53," said Chad, taking a quick look at the boarding passes, confirming their numbers, before handing Bill his. "I guess I won't have time to charge the phone." Seven minutes later they were lining up with all the other 'B' passengers. Ten minutes later they were boarding and twenty-five minutes after that it was wheels up and they were heading back to the dry heat of the Las Vegas Valley.

"Almost four and a half hours."

"What's that, Chad?"

"Four Hours and twenty eight minutes flight time. We've got a long flight in front of us."

"So, what's the damage?" Bill asked.

"The damage? I assume you're referring to our nest egg and our withdrawal plan now that we have spent over $35,000 helping my mother with her medical bills and ensuring that she could stay in her house," Chad confirmed.

"Yep. What are we looking at with respect to our nest egg and our plan for retirement income."

"I don't know yet to tell you the truth," Chad confided, "I have given it some thought but I won't know specifics until we get home and I run the numbers through a few calculators and update our financial planning spreadsheet. Until then I won't know how our new withdrawal plan will shake out."

"So what are the considerations?" Bill asked.

"Don't tell me you've forgot?" said Chad, chiding Bill. "We've had this conversation multiple times."

"Humor me. Tell me again."

"Most withdrawal plans are based on the 4% rule. In general, the rule says that if retirees take out 4% of their nest egg the first year in retirement, and then adjust that rate to account for inflation in each subsequent year, they will not run out of money for at least three decades. As an example, if inflation increases 1% during the first year of retirement, 5% would be taken out during the second year in retirement. Conversely, if inflation decreases 1% during the first year of retirement, 3% would be taken out during the second year in retirement."

"That makes sense," said Bill.

Chad continued. "The 4% number was originally based on a portfolio with a 60/40 split between large-cap stocks and intermediate-term government bonds. However, after research, William Bengen, the founder of the rule, decided to add small-cap stocks to the mix and revised his recommendation to 4.5%. However, for whatever reasons, the 4% name stuck. While some believe the 4% is simply too arbitrary, some believe it is too high, and some believe too low, it provides a good starting point for most people."

"So we've been using the 4% rule as the foundation for how much money we withdraw from our retirement accounts each year?"

"Yes and no."

"Yes and no?"

"Since the two of us are only 58, we are not currently drawing money from our 401(k) and IRA retirement accounts. Withdrawals from those accounts can't start without penalty before age 59½. However, our withdrawal plan is based on the 4% rule."

"You referenced the 59½ age requirement; so what if money is withdrawn before 59½?"

"Taking money out early from a retirement plan can cost an individual an extra 10% in taxes. However, the additional 10% tax normally does not apply to nontaxable withdrawals."

"Nontaxable withdrawals?"

"Nontaxable withdrawals include withdrawals of the cost of participating in a plan; and the cost includes contributions that an individual paid tax on before they put them into the plan. Also, if someone transfers a withdrawal from one qualified retirement plan to another within 60 days, the transfer is considered a rollover and rollovers are not subject to income tax. In short, the added 10% tax also does not apply to a rollover. There are several other exceptions to the additional 10%, such as withdrawals if an individual has certain medical expenses or if they are disabled."

"That seems to be a lot to consider."

"It can be. Also, it has to be remembered that the withdrawal rate isn't the only factor. The order of withdrawal from the various retirement accounts is also critical."

"What do you mean?"

"For most people, taxable accounts, such as brokerage accounts, are withdrawn first as they are generally taxed at favorable dividend and capital gains rates and only on the capital appreciation. In fact, our brokerage and money market accounts are where we have been drawing our money since we retired 15 months ago. We've just been using those accounts and my pension from the Air Force up to this point. After withdrawals from taxable accounts, the order is generally from tax-deferred accounts such as 401(k) accounts and Traditional IRAs; and finally, tax exempt accounts such as Roth IRAs. Now that we took out that significant amount of money from my brokerage account, money that I was not planning on spending, I need to reassess how we draw down the money remaining in our brokerage and money market accounts between now and the time we each turn 59½."

"The bottom line is this, we are not currently employing the 4% rule. However, our withdrawal plan is currently based on a 4% withdrawal rate once we do start withdrawals from our retirement accounts. A quick side note, I am giving some thought to using a 3 - 3½% withdrawal rate instead of 4%."

"That means we'll be drawing out less money from our retirement accounts each year. Correct?" asked Bill.

"Yep. That's right."

"As I said, I have given some thought to how the recent expenditure of the $35,000 will impact us but I won't know the specifics of how we might make adjustments to our withdrawal plan until we get home and I run the numbers through a few calculators, looking at the impact of various withdrawal rates and update our financial planning spreadsheet. My pension from the Air Force and our Social Security pensions will also factor into how much we need to draw from our various retirement accounts. As you correctly noted, there is a lot to consider."

Landing at McCarran, right on schedule, Bill and Chad made their way to Terminal 1 – Economy Parking after picking up their checked bags. It had been a long day and they were anxious to get home. Leaving McCarran, they jumped on I-215 South, traveling quickly to South Eastern Avenue which delivered them to their Sun City Anthem community.

"Is that your phone?" Bill asked a semi-comatose Chad, upon hearing the slightest noise made by a vibrating phone. Reaching instinctively into his pocket, Chad pulled out his phone, which he thought was dead, to check his latest text message: *from Vallory – Dave and Mary are hosting a cookout Saturday hope you made it home safely.* Chad considered just waiting until the morning to reply as he didn't want to get drawn into a long text exchange;

he was far too tired. However, it looked like he had just enough juice left in his phone for a message and he did want their friend to know they had made it home safely: *to Vallory – just landed on the way home talk tomorrow.*

[2] SUMMER DAYS

Stepping out their front door, Dave and Mary stretched quickly. They had intended to run a little bit earlier but they had unexpectedly overslept. Now it was 6:50 a.m. and the temperature had already climbed to 74 degrees.

"So much for getting out by 5:45 and beatin' the heat," Dave moaned.

"Suck it up, Honey, we'll be alright," Mary encouraged him. With the brief stretches out of the way they took off at an easy pace, settling into a nice rhythm, about an 8:45 per mile pace after the first $\frac{1}{4}$ mile. Though warmer than desired, it was a beautiful morning and it felt good to be up and active. Heading down Hampton Road they planned to make a left on Anthem Parkway and head toward Sun City Anthem Drive and complete their regular $3\frac{1}{2}$ mile loop.

Turning left on Sun City Anthem Drive they passed George and Sandra running the opposite way.

"Good morning, guys," Dave called out, "see you Saturday at the house."

"I'll call ya later, Mary," Sandra called out, "let me know if you need me to bring something."

"Sounds good," Mary shouted out as George and Sandra drifted further away. Making their way west on Sun City Anthem Drive, with the sun on their backs, Mary could feel the its warmth bearing down on her shoulder blades.

"How ya feeling, Babe?" George asked.

"Not too bad. Although I should have put a little sunscreen on this morning." Picking up the pace for the last $\frac{1}{8}$ mile, both were sweating profusely by the time their home came into view. Passing their home they settled into a shuffle which eventually became a walk.

"Walk for a $\frac{1}{2}$ mile or so to cool down?" asked Mary.

"Sounds good to me. Considering the heat I don't know if our core temperature will come down much anytime soon, but it is a good to walk and stretch out the muscles."

"True," Mary laughed. "I don't know that it is possible to 'cool down' in the Nevada desert after a run, no matter the time of day."

"We need to get to the store sometime today to pick up stuff for the cookout. How about we get cleaned up as soon as we get back to the house, I make you some breakfast and then we head to the grocery store while it's still early," suggested Dave. "Do what we can to beat the crowd."

"Sounds good, Honey," replied Mary. "I know how much you hate shopping, particularly when you have to contend with aisles full of people. Also, remember my nephew Paul is coming by this afternoon to update the software on that stupid computer and to see if he can figure out why we keep dropping our Wi-Fi connection."

Half a block from their home Dave and Mary ran into their next door neighbors, Tom and Kim.

"Howdy, neighbors," Dave greeted them as they drew closer. "How was your trip? Alaska correct?"

"It was Alaska and it was a great trip!" Tom informed them. Just got back a couple of days ago. We did the sea & land tour; four days on land and seven on the sea. We spent some time in Fairbanks mining for gold and sailing down the Chena River. We also spent a day at Denali Park. Beautiful. Absolutely beautiful. Been there?"

"No. Not yet. But our friend Charles was stationed there in the Army and he has nothing but praise. How was the sea cruise?" Mary asked.

"Loved it. We left from Seward, near Anchorage, and cruised to Vancouver, stopping at four different ports along the way," Kim said, "engaging in different shore excursions."

"I've heard those are great, which was your favorite?" inquired Mary.

"Probably the helicopter ride to the Hubbard glacier. Phenomenal. Absolutely phenomenal!"

"I bet."

"So what happened with the Colorado State University football coach?" Dave asked. Of course he knew. As a University of Colorado alum however, he just wanted to needle Tom a little.

"I was just reading about that," replied Tom. Apparently, the head coach just resigned after it was revealed that he knew and concealed from the NCAA that several star players had received financial benefits from selling sporting memorabilia and received discounts on purchases of clothes, tattoos and cars. Hopefully they will find a new coach soon and move on, get their house in order."

"We'll see," said Dave. "We'll see. Well, we need to get to the house and get cleaned up after our run. Enjoy your walk and we'll talk to you guys later."

After enjoying her breakfast of scrambled eggs, bacon and some toast, Vallory set about preparing her coffee. The first order of business was to fill the maker with four cups of cold, charcoal-filtered water. Next, two heaping scoops of her current preference, Kikai Kenya from Lexington

Coffee Roasters. Turning the coffee pot on, she grabbed her mug adding one teaspoon of sugar - none of that fake, cancer inducing imitation stuff - and one tablespoon of heavy whipping cream. It was the routine she performed every morning. As the intense and pungent aroma of fresh-cut fir, plum blossom and black currant began to waft throughout the house she gathered her latest checking, savings and investment statements.

Once the coffee was finished brewing she poured the black liquid into her favorite mug and watched as it morphed into a caramel colored nectar. "Ah, perfection," she whispered to herself as she made her way to the den. Sitting down in front of her computer, she set the coffee mug down, grabbed the mouse and opened up Quicken. While she faithfully updated Quicken on a regular basis, to account for daily purchases and monthly bills, she put a special emphasis on conducting a thorough update and review every quarter when she received her investment statements for each of her respective investment accounts.

Saving the largest, most significant account for last, Vallory opened the envelope containing her BFSG statement. She had to check the date on the statement twice as the balance was exactly the same as last quarter, $745,934.25. It had to be a typographical mistake considering the odds against ending two consecutive quarters with exactly the same balance; and the fact that Carl Morrison and BFSG had delivered consistent 6 - 7% monthly returns in the two years since she moved the bulk of her investments to the small boutique. Unfortunately, as a small boutique investment advisory firm, only a listing of their services and contact information were available on their website. Services such as viewing and downloading statements were not yet available. *No big deal*, she thought, *I'll just give Carl a call.* Making her way back to the kitchen, where she had left her cell phone, she picked it up off the counter and dialed the number for the BFSG office.

"Good morning. BFSG, how may I assist you?"

"Darlene?"

"Yes. Yes it is."

"Good morning, Darlene. This is Vallory Jackson. How are you?"

"I'm well, Ms. Jackson and yourself?"

"No complaints. Every day above ground is a good day. Can I speak with Carl please?"

"Certainly, Ms. Jackson. Just one moment please."

Picking up after a brief minute, Carl came on the line and was his normal, jovial self. If he was a superhero, he would probably be Captain Positivity. *I suppose that type of personality is a must in his line of work*, Vallory thought. Vallory often felt uplifted after speaking with Carl.

"Good morning, Val. How are you this fine morning?"
"I'm well, Carl. Yourself?"
"I'm good. A beautiful day today. Thanks. How can I be of service?"
Vallory explained the apparent error for which Carl apologized profusely.
"I'm so sorry to inconvenience you, Val. We had a problem with our computer system last week and some of the client records did not update accurately. However, that has been fixed and I will ensure an updated, correct copy of your statement gets placed in the mail today. Does that sound okay?"
"Perfect, Carl. Thank you so much."
"Not a problem. Don't hesitate to call me if you have any questions after you get the correct statement. Take care and have a good weekend."
"Thanks, Carl. You too." Putting her paperwork away and closing Excel, she made a mental note to finish updating her documents and concluding her monthly review once she got the updated statement from Morrison.

Reaching high into the cupboard next to the refrigerator, Charles pulled out his blender. He wanted to get a good swim in later this morning so a light, quick breakfast was in order. His signature Green Machine smoothie would be just right. *So what's going on with the stock market and the economy?* he thought to himself as he reached for the remote, turned the TV on and changed the channel to Bloomberg TV. Some host he had never seen before was moderating a panel discussing retiring into a bear market:

> Host: "So get us up to speed. What constitutes a bear market?"
>
> First Guest: "Bear markets are defined as a decline in the S&P 500 Index of at least 20 percent from the previous high. They happen fairly frequently, happening on average, about every three years over the last 80 years, with an average decline of about 35 percent."
>
> Second Guest: "So for all the talk of 2008 - 2009 being the 'worst recession since the Great Depression,' the S&P 500 losing 37 percent in 2008 was incredibly close to that average decline. Even with this in mind, it seems that we, as investors, are surprised every time there is a market correction or bear market."

> Host: "So what should viewers nearing retirement do to avoid being gouged by the bear market?"
>
> Second Guest: "They should consider meeting with a financial planner or CPA to discuss their numbers and formulate a plan for retirement. Also, they should calculate their 'hurdle rate,' their personal minimum rate of return needed to meet their retirement goals. This is more important than any index return. If their hurdle rate is 3 percent, they should be fine. If their hurdle rate is 15 percent, they should probably reevaluate their anticipated retirement date and goals."
>
> First Guest: "I would add that folks should create a disciplined investment and distribution plan to protect against downturns, remove emotional reactions to market declines and determine ahead of time what the plan is in terms of spending during a market downturn."

As the talking heads on TV droned on, he grabbed the ingredients for his smoothie: a banana, raw spinach, a green apple, a little broccoli, half an avocado, ice and some protein powder. After giving the mixture a 30-second blend he poured the velvety smooth drink into a tall glass, grabbed a straw and plopped down on the sofa in the living room.

> Host: "Thanks to the both of you for joining us this morning. After the break, Karen speaks with Paul Franklin, a retiree making the most of his golden years."

Quickly changing the channel during the commercial break, he wanted to see what the weather was supposed to be like over the next couple days. According to Prime Weather, Henderson could expect a high today near 93, southeast winds around 6 mph; tonight mostly clear, with a low around 73. For Saturday, south southwest wind 6 to 10 mph and mostly sunny with a high near 94. *Sound like good cookout weather*, Charles thought to himself as he flipped the TV back to Bloomberg. His favorite host, Karen McDonald, was speaking to the guest who had recently retired:

> Karen : "My guest, Paul Franklin, retired in January 2014, a few months after his wife passed away. The couple, who raised four children, were living in Arizona at the time and planned on selling their home and living out their golden years traveling around the country in an RV. He has spent

the last eight months exploring the Southwestern part of the country. Thanks for joining us, Paul. After your wife passed, you decided to stick with your original plan of traveling around the country in an RV."

Paul: "That's right. After my wife passed I just wanted to get away after working for more than 42 years in the telecommunications industry. I was more determined than ever to carry out our plans."

Karen: "Sounds great. You also owned some rental properties, correct?"

Paul: "Yes, we had two rental properties. When I retired I quickly sold them along with our primary residence and most of our belongings. The proceeds helped fund my nest egg. After raising four children into our 50s, it wasn't quite as large as I would have hoped."

Karen: "So in addition to your Social Security income, how much do you have in savings?"

Paul: "Just over $226,000. I set up an account where I could withdraw money from my CDs each year and I use that along with my Social Security income."

Paul went on, praising the value of saving early and consistently; and having a plan in place before you retire, lest you find yourself at home alone and bored. Peeling himself off the sofa 40 minutes later, Charles headed to his bedroom to get changed. Twenty minutes later he was out the door, headed to Liberty Center to get in 45 minutes of lap swimming.

Following a three-mile walk in the morning and breakfast at The Cracked Egg, over on North Green Valley Parkway, Chad and Bill returned home and got right to work; Bill with cleaning the house and Chad with reassessing their withdrawal plan. Four and a half hours later, long after Bill had finished his housework and fallen asleep watching television in the living room, Chad emerged from the den.

"Hey, Sleepyhead," Chad called out as he came into the living room and gently shook Bill, waking him from his slumber. "All finished and we're in good shape. Better than I would have thought."

"Well that's good to know," Bill managed to communicate between two deep yawns and a stretch. "Are we still on track for a retirement income of $102,000 annually?"

"Yep. The only thing we need to do now is move $125,000 from our BFSG account to our checking account. That will be the money we use between now and the time you turn 59½ and start withdrawals from your 401(k). I'm going to call Morrison now, before the weekend, and let him know we want to make that withdrawal."

"Sounds good to me."

After the fifth ring Chad was just about to hang up when Carl picked up the phone. Momentarily confused, Chad finally spoke. "I'm sorry, Carl. This is Chad. Chad Richardson. I was just about to hang up and then I was expecting to hear Darlene on the other end. I was thrown off for a moment."

"Not a problem, Chad. Darlene has left for the day, and in fact, I was just about to close the office. You caught me just in time. How are you?"

"I'm well."

"And Bill?"

"Not too bad. Hey, Carl, we've recently had some unexpected expenditures, dealing with my mom in Florida ... "

"I hope she's okay," Carl offered.

"Yes, she'll be fine. As I was saying, we've recently had some unexpected expenditures and after looking at each of our accounts and running the numbers, I'm going to need $125,000 from our investment account."

"Not a problem, Chad. I will have a check cut for you on Monday. Will that work for you?"

"Sounds good, Carl. Thanks and have a great weekend."

"You do the same, Chad and give Bill my best. And by the way, when am I going to have a chance to meet Bill?" I believe the last time you guys came by the office to drop off paperwork I was out."

"You were. Maybe we can get together for lunch or something soon?"

"Sounds good. I'll schedule something with Darlene."

After Chad hung up, Bill asked, "Have you talked to Vallory yet?"

"What for?"

"To find out what time we're supposed to be at the cookout tomorrow."

"Oh yeah, that's right. Let me give her a call real quick."

After lunch, Sandra grabbed all the mail from the last two days and sat down in the den, methodically separating the junk, which was most of it, from the stuff she wanted to take a closer look at.

"What are you doing?" George called out from the kitchen as he finished washing up the last of the dishes.

"Just going through the mail, Hon." After opening up the statement from BFSG she signed out of her email account and minimized the browser window on the computer and opened up the spreadsheet where she maintained all of the information relating to their savings and investment accounts; which allowed her to effectively manage their finances.

"Well that's weird," she said out loud.

"What's that, Babe?" George yelled from the kitchen.

"I said, that's weird."

"What's weird?" George asked as he stepped into the den with a dish towel slung over his shoulder.

"I was just looking at our quarterly statement from BFSG and the balance is exactly the same as it was last quarter."

"That is odd," George concurred. "I'll bet it's just a typo or something."

"You're probably right. I'll just give Carl a call," she said, reaching into her pocket for her cell phone.

"Hmm, not there," she said to herself. "I must have left it in the bedroom. Getting up from the desk, she made her way upstairs to the bedroom. Walking into the kitchen, where George was working feverishly to remove a sticky mess from the counter, she started to dial the number for the BFSG office. "On second thought, I'll just wait until Monday," she informed her husband. "Carl can be a little too talkative and I don't want to get bogged down in a long conversation. I have too much I want to get done this afternoon."

"Sounds like a plan, wife."

"Thanks, husband. Every once in a while I have a good idea. Need some help over there?"

"I just might," George said laughing. "Something has hardened on the counter and doesn't want to come off."

Scrambling to get ready before the gang arrived, Dave lit the grill only to have it go out four minutes later. "Doggit!" he yelled out after giving the tank a firm shake. "We're out of propane."

"Not a problem, Babe. We have about 15 minutes before people start arriving. You've got some time to go pick up another tank." Just then the doorbell rang.

"Or maybe not," said Dave. "I'm going to head out real quick and grab one."

"Sounds good. You do that and I'll get the door and keep everyone entertained until you get back." Quickly grabbing his keys, Dave headed for the garage.

"Glad you guys could make it," said Mary as she greeted Bill and Chad with big, soulful hugs. "How was the flight home?"

"It was good. A long flight, but good. I'm so glad to get home and out of that humidity," Bill said, "it was killin' me!"

"I bet. Well welcome home. It really is good to see you guys."

"Well it is good to be seen," Chad quickly deadpanned.

"And your mom? I understand she is doing better."

"She is. Still feisty as hell, but definitely doing better."

"Good. So glad to hear it. Well come on in and get comfortable, make yourselves at home. There's beer and wine out back if you need something to wet your whistle and some finger foods if you need something to snack on." Just as she started to close the door Charles came into view.

"Well good afternoon, Mr. Bingman," she said waving. "Come on in and join the party."

"Hello, Mary, how are ya? Where's your old man?" he asked as he bent slightly, giving Mary a hug and a peck on the cheek.

"I'm good. Dave had to run over to Home Depot and grab a propane tank. Turns out the one we had was on the last of its fumes."

"He should have called. I always keep a second tank on standby just in case. The first time I ran out of propane with guests waiting was the last time. Keeping a second tank can help you avoid a lot of aggravation. Trust me."

"That's exactly what we should do. We've talked about it but never gotten around to just doing it. You know what ... " Grabbing her phone she sent a text: *to Dave - pick up two tanks we'll keep one on standby.* Seconds later came his reply: *to Mary - that's a good idea. will do.*

Fifteen minutes later George, Sandra and Vallory arrived together just as Dave pulled into the driveway and made his way into the open garage, creeping along slowly, ensuring that he didn't side swipe their golf cart. "I really wish we had bought a house with a 2½ car garage," he mumbled to himself. "It definitely would have been more convenient." Bringing the car to a stop, he jumped out after hitting the switch to open the trunk.

"What do you got there?" George asked, breaking away from his wife and Vallory as he shuffled into the garage.

"Hey there, George. How are ya, buddy?"

"Doing well. If I was any better I wouldn't be able to stand myself."

"I hear ya. I had to run to the store, Home Depot, and pick up a propane tank. As fate would have it, the one we had was near empty. I should have thought about checking it yesterday."

"Need a hand?"

"In fact I do. I went ahead and picked up two tanks, that way we'll always have one on standby." While the men grabbed the tanks, Mary escorted Sandra and Vallory to the backyard where everyone was gathered.

"Can I assume that is a cheesecake?" Mary asked Sandra, spying the covered dish.

"It is. Just a little something I whipped up real quick," she said, giving her friend a slight wink.

"Sorry, everyone," said Dave, as he went about hooking up the propane tank. "I beg for your forgiveness. We're going to eat a little bit later. Unfortunately, Mary forgot to check the propane tank yesterday."

"Hey!" Mary cried out, "don't blame me."

"I had to blame someone. I hate to keep these good people, and Charles, waiting."

"Very funny," laughed Charles. "You are quite the comedian."

"I know everyone is anxiously awaiting dinner and I'm looking forward to trying out a new grilled bologna recipe."

"I was so excited thinking about the bologna I didn't eat breakfast this morning," said Vallory. "I wanted to make sure I brought an empty stomach and ravenous appetite to this soirée."

"Bring on the bologna," Sandra chimed in.

Twenty minutes later the steaks and chicken were off the grill and the sides, a veritable smorgasbord of goodness, were set out. As the sun dipped below the horizon and late into the September evening, the gang of eight partook of food, drink and conversation, concluding the evening with cups of coffee and the cheesecake, brought by Sandra. The group had agreed long ago that she made the finest cheesecake any of them had ever eaten. Being the baker of the finest known cheesecake meant that she was obliged to bring her cheesecake to each and every group gathering of course. "That cheesecake was heavenly," said Vallory.

"Why thank you, Val," replied Sandra. "I'm glad you enjoyed it."

"A great dessert following a great meal," said Charles. Raising his own glass, he waited as his friends grabbed theirs. "To Mary and Dave for hosting such a fine shindig, and to friendship. 'It is the source of the greatest pleasures, and without friends even the most agreeable pursuits become tedious.'"

"Mahatma Gandhi?" guessed Bill.

"Nope," replied Charles.

"Mark Twain," guessed Mary.

"No."

"Stephen King," said Chad, laughing.

"Definitely not Mr. King," Charles said, "although I love his work."

"St. Thomas Aquinas," Vallory offered authoritatively. "The Italian friar, priest, influential philosopher and theologian."

"Right you are, Val," said Charles as they each raised their glass.

"To friendship!" they proclaimed in unison.

After bidding their goodbyes, Vallory joined Sandra and George in the short walk to their homes.

"Another great evening with some great friends," George mused.

"Absolutely," agreed Vallory.

"What are you doing tomorrow, Val?" Sandra inquired. "Nothing. After tonight, I will probably sleep till noon. You know me, I'm usually in bed by 9:30 or so. What time is it, George?"

"11:26, my friend."

"Oh yeah, I'll definitely be sleeping in." The friends walked along in silence for a while, enjoying the cool desert air and the comfort offered by the silence.

"How about you guys?" Vallory asked, breaking the silence. "Any plans?"

"Same thing probably. I don't think we have any plans specific for tomorrow and not much on Monday" said Sandra.

"Yep, nothing much on Monday outside of calling Carl over at BFSG and check on that quarterly statement."

"What's up with your quarterly statement?" asked Vallory.

"I was reviewing our investment accounts earlier today and noticed that the balance was exactly the same as last quarter; down to the penny," said Sandra.

"Mine too," Vallory said, "so I called Carl yesterday."

"Yours too? What did he say?"

"Something about a problem with their computer system last week and some of the client records did not update accurately. But he said it had been fixed. He's supposed to send me an updated, correct statement."

"I figured it was something like that," said George.

"I'll just call Monday and have them send the updated statement," said Sandra as she struggled to stifle a yawn.

"Sounds good, wife."

[3] REVELATIONS

Thursday morning. Finishing up their round at the Concord, Vallory and Sandra headed straight to Buckman's Grille where a couple of cold beers awaited them. "Not a bad round, girlfriend," said Sandra as they settled into their seats at the bar.

"Definitely better than last week. At least I drove it more consistently this morning," replied Vallory. "Hey, I meant to ask you, did you and George ever get the correct copy of your quarterly statement from Carl over at BFSG?"

"We did," Sandra said, "it came in the mail yesterday afternoon. How about you. Did you get yours?"

"I did. It came in Tuesday's mail."

"I love the consistent returns ... "

"Absolutely."

"That sounds like your ... " Sandra started to say as her own phone vibrated in her pocket.

Reaching her phone first, Vallory read the text out loud: *from Chad - four tickets to Michael Jackson ONE tomorrow night interested?*

"Yep," Sandra said, checking her phone, "I got the same message. That sounds fun. Want to go?"

"Absolutely," said Vallory.

"Just reply for us both," suggested Sandra.

Vallory quickly pounded out a reply: *to Chad - sounds great Sandra and I are definitely in.*

"Have you been following that story out of Newark and the pension problems there?" Vallory asked.

"A little bit. Why do you ask?"

"In general because I think we are going to see a lot more municipalities, and corporations, reduce pension benefits and shed their responsibilities related to paying pension benefits; and specifically because I have a cousin, Linda, who retired as a city employee from the Newark Housing Department, that is being impacted."

"How long has she been retired?"

"Seven, almost eight years."

"So what is the status? I did read something about ongoing negotiations."

"Yep, that's where it's at. Right now the two unions - who represent most of the retirees and current city workers - and the lawyers for the city of Newark are trying to hammer out an agreement. I believe they plan to negotiate for another two weeks. If they can't reach an agreement, the city has threatened to file for bankruptcy, potentially leaving retirees and current workers with nothing. The last time I spoke to her, the city was offering 42 cents on the dollar for current retirees, advocating that the contribution level for current employees be increased from 3% to 6.5% and that medical benefits essentially be cut in half for current and future retirees."

"Yikes. That sounds pretty draconian."

"It does. Linda is a little nervous because she basically relies on just her pension check form the city and Social Security. The proposed changes would significantly impact her standard of living ... "

"And it isn't as if she can just go out and pick up another job."

"Exactly. Like us, she ain't no spring chicken."

"She told me that one of her greatest frustrations is the way the city's lawyers and some pundits try to frame the issue. As she told me, a lot of people believe, incorrectly, that all government employees are getting sweetheart pensions from their former big salaries and enjoying early retirements. However, she didn't retire until she was 63 and as she put it, the vast majority of Newark's 17,000 or so retirees receive modest monthly stipends derived from decades of public service patrolling streets, putting out fires, running crucial city departments and saving lives. Her pension is only $1,018 a month; not exactly a princely sum.

They were not the ones who made poor investment choices or overpromised on benefits. However, there is no doubt that they will be made to feel the pain from Newark's forced financial restructuring, especially those who didn't pay into Social Security and have nothing else, or those who rely on the current level of medical benefits as their only health care safety net."

"What happens if it goes to the courts?"

"No one is sure. The unions believe that the city cannot file for bankruptcy if it includes reducing pension benefits for retired workers, benefits specifically protected in the New Jersey State Constitution. However, Chapter 9 bankruptcy is governed by federal law. The city's lawyers would likely argue that federal law trumps any state constitutional guarantees concerning the retirement benefits."

"Well, I certainly hope things work out for her and the other retirees."

"Me too. I feel so bad for her."

Friday night. "Well, what can you say about the Las Vegas strip at night that probably hasn't already been said?"

"Nothing," Chad quickly replied.

"Ha-ha," Bill laughed sarcastically, giving Chad a look. "I've lived here for eight years and I'm still blown away by the neon lights and people; the energy emanating from both is absolutely palpable."

"At my age I need to draw all the energy I can ... from wherever I can," cracked Vallory. "Particularly for the later shows."

"I almost had four tickets for the 7:30 p.m. show but it sold out at the last minute. But look on the bright side, we got great seats," noted Chad.

"That were free," Sandra added.

"Exactly. So who's your friend, Chad?" asked Vallory.

"Her name is Loretta. We worked together years ago in Boulder. She's been here in Vegas about a year and recently got hired as a production manager."

"Nice."

"*Michael Jackson ONE* should be good," Bill said, "I know you've seen a couple of the Cirque du Soleil shows, Val ... "

"Three of 'em: *Ka*, *Mystère* and *O*. Loved them all, especially *Mystère*."

"So what about you, Sandra? Seen any of the shows?"

"Nope. I'm a Cirque du Soleil virgin."

There's a joke in there somewhere, thought Vallory.

"Don't even say whatever it is you're thinking," warned Sandra, raising a balled fist. "I can see the wheels spinning in that head of yours and I know you too well."

"Who me?" asked Vallory, feigning ignorance.

"Yes you. You know that I definitely know you too well."

"Well, you are in for a treat, girl."

"I certainly hope so."

"I did read some reviews when I heard you got tickets, Chad. I've always been a Michael Jackson fan. Most of them were positive. We'll see."

"Yes we will," agreed Vallory. "As long as we don't fall asleep." Just as their taxi pulled up to the Mandalay Bay, Sandra did all she could to contain a yawn.

"Uh oh, you better suck in some of that Vegas energy," encouraged Vallory. Laughing, Vallory paid the driver as they exited the cab and headed for the front entrance.

"What do we owe you?" asked Bill.

"Nothing, Honey. You got the tickets to the show."

"Well that works for me."

Making their way to the theatre, Vallory asked Sandra about George. "What is your husband up to tonight?"

"I guess Mary was going to play dominoes over at the Anthem Center so Dave was going to join George and Charles and enjoy a boy's night out at some cigar bar, the West World or something?"

"The West Wing Cigar Lounge over on South Durango Drive. It's supposed to be a pretty swanky joint."

"That's it. He said they were going to enjoy some scotch and hand rolled cigars tonight."

Two or three times a year the guys liked to enjoy a testosterone laden night out. Cigar bars, like the West Wing or En Fuego Cigars & Lounge over on West Sahara Avenue, were their favorite escapes and provided the perfect environment for relaxing, good conversation and enjoying the company of good friends. Smoking a quality hand rolled cigar with a stiff drink, or two, was a great way to spend an evening. Every time he walked through the doors of the West Wing, the aromatic blend of freshly cut grass and roasted hazelnuts, carried in a cloud of smoke, washed over Charles. Tonight was no different and he inhaled deeply and exhaled slowly as the three friends made their way past the bar and to a table.

"Too bad Bill and Chad couldn't join us tonight, but I'm sure they'll have a good time at the Cirque du Soleil show. Those are usually pretty good," said Dave as they sat down.

"Yeah, I know Chad really appreciates a good cigar. They'll probably make the next night out," suggested Charles as he raised his hand slightly in an attempt to get the attention of one of the wait staff. One of the waitresses, with jet black hair, beautiful toffee colored skin and a radiant smile, caught the movement out of the corner of her eye and quickly made her way to their table.

"Good evening, gentlemen, my name is Cherie, I'll be taking care of you this evening. Can I start you off with drinks?"

"Yes you may," replied Charles. "The Highland Park Scotch."

"Neat?"

"Just a touch of soft still spring water, please."

"The same," said Dave.

"And you, sir?" she asked George.

"The Highland Park, neat. Thank you, Cherie."

"Thank you, gentlemen. Will you be smoking with us this evening."

"Absolutely," the three friends replied in unison.

"Let me get your drinks and I will return momentarily to take your order."

"I've always drank my scotch neat," said George. "Why the soft still spring water, Charles?"

"My experience has been that water can enhance the aroma and flavor and bring out some of the hidden characteristics. However, you have to be mindful. Regular tap water can contain high levels of chlorine which will spoil rather than complement the whisky, that's why I always make sure to specify a soft still spring water."

"What about ice?" Dave asked.

"I occasionally add ice, which can be refreshing, particularly if it is a warmer evening. However, my experience has been that ice does dull the aromas and taste slightly. I have also noticed that carbonated water, which I have tried a couple times, will also interfere with the aromas. I would never say there is a 'right' way or a 'wrong' way to drink whisky, but the addition of mixers such as ginger ale, soda or a cola, is a growing trend, however it does beg the question, why drink whisky at all if you need to mask the taste?"

"Interesting," said Dave. "Great food for thought."

"Agreed," said George, as he spied Cherie approaching with their drinks. "I'll have to try a drink with spring water sometime ... and ensure I avoid carbonated mixers."

"Highland Park Scotch all around," said Cherie. "One neat for you, sir," as she placed the first tumbler, filled with the caramel colored libation, in front of George. "And two with soft still spring water, for you gentlemen. Our spotlight cigar this week is the Arturo Fuente Opus X BBMF Natural Perfecto 2013, an exceptionally fragrant stick that offers a floral aroma complemented by a mild spice on the finish."

"That sounds wonderful, Cherie," Dave assured her. "However, I believe we'll start with three of the Nestor Miranda Domincano sticks. We've heard a lot about it and have been looking forward to giving it a try."

"A good choice. I enjoyed one with my boyfriend a few months ago."

"Oh really? How was the flavor?" inquired Charles.

"Nice. As I recall, the initial puff was somewhat earthy with a hint of nuts and a just a bit of spiciness. After the first third, the stick produced a warmer spice, somewhat sweet, and the tobacco seemed to become a bit more complex. I really enjoyed it."

"Sounds good. Bring them on."

"Great, I will be back with your sticks shortly. In the meantime, please enjoy your drinks."

"Both of you have accounts with Carlton Morrison over at BFSG, correct?" Dave asked Charles and George.

"Yep," Charles replied as George nodded in the affirmative.

"Are you happy with his services and the returns you've been getting? I currently have most of my money with Fidelity but I'm considering making a move. I'm thinking a smaller, local boutique might offer some advantages with respect to more personalized service." George answered first.

"Yes and no. Yes in that the returns have been very consistent and that is definitely a priority for me in retirement. At this point in my life I am most interested in protecting my money and ensuring that I can draw a consistent income stream from my investments."

"Why, no?"

"No in that I'm a little disappointed, no, make that perplexed, that in the twenty-first century I can't manage my accounts online. The only thing really offered via the BFSG website is the ability to view a listing of their services and contact information. Services such as viewing and downloading statements are not available. At least not at this time."

"Hmm, that is odd," mused Dave.

"I understand that they're a smaller boutique operation, but the ability to review and manage accounts online seems like a basic service that would be offered," said Dave.

"Exactly. As an example, when Sandra and I got our latest quarterly statement, last week, she noticed that the balance was exactly the same as the previous quarter. It would have been nice to be able to go online and review the history of the account and download statements or other relevant information. Instead, Sandra had to call over to BFSG on Monday and speak directly to Carl."

"What was the issue?"

"He said that ... "

"Let me guess," interrupted Charles. "He said there was some kind of problem with their computer system the previous week and some of the client records did not update accurately. However, the system had been fixed since then and he would send you an updated, correct statement."

"Exactly," said George. "Almost verbatim. How did you know?"

"That is the exact same thing he said happened to my statement last quarter, three months ago, and the same explanation he gave me."

"Fantastic show," Bill raved, turning his phone on as they streamed out of the theatre with the other patrons of the show. His phone immediately notified him of three e-mails.

"That really was great," agreed Vallory. "Thank you so much for the tickets and thinking of me."

"Absolutely," agreed Sandra. That was fantastic. I'm already mentally making plans to see another show, with George."

"I'm glad you guys enjoyed it. Let's hustle over to the taxi stand, try to beat some of this crowd," said Chad as he pulled out his phone and sent a quick text message to his friend and former co-worker: *to Loretta - just left the show fantastic! thanks and we'll talk soon.*

"What the fu ... " Bill started to say.

"What's wrong, Babe?" Chad asked.

"Just saw an e-mail from the bank. Apparently the electronic funds transfer I tried to make for the mortgage payment was rejected for non-sufficient funds."

"What? Non-sufficient funds. We just deposited that check we got from Carl at BFSG. There should be plenty of money. More than enough to cover the mortgage."

"I know. Hold on. I'm logging into the bank account now and trying to find out what's going on."

"Here we go," Vallory informed the group as they had made their way to the front of the taxi queue and the next taxi pulled to a stop in front of them. The four friends quickly jumped in and they were off, on their way home.

"Here we go," said Bill. "What day did we get the check from BFSG?"

"Monday. No, Tuesday," answered Chad.

"That's right 'cause I deposited it Wednesday morning," mumbled Bill as he looked down and scrolled through their bank transactions on his phone. Hmm."

"What?" Chad asked.

"Yep, I deposited it on Wednesday but it never cleared. It looks like the BFSG account which the check was written against, from Bank of the West, contained insufficient funds."

"Hold on," Sandra said, "I don't mean to poke my nose into your business, but we all have money with BFSG. Are you saying that a check you received from Carl Morrison at BFSG bounced?"

"Yep," answered Bill. "That would appear to be the case."

"Well that is a little disconcerting," said Vallory, speaking up.

"George and Sandra, and I, just had an interesting experience with BFSG."

"What was that?" Chad asked.

"Well, we got our quarterly statement last week," said Sandra.

"Yep, so did we," noted Bill.

"Was there anything odd about your statement?" asked Vallory.

"Not that I recall," answered Bill with a quizzical look on his face as he looked at Chad. "Everything seemed fine to me. The gains and the account balance seemed right in line with what they should have been. I'll have to check again when we get home though. Why? What was odd about your statements?"

"The balance on the quarterly statement was exactly the same as the balance from the statement three months prior," said Sandra.

"Exactly the same?" asked Chad.

"Exactly. Down to the last penny."

"That is odd," said Bill.

"Yep," Vallory said, "so George and Sandra did what I did. They called and spoke to Carl."

"What did Morrison have to say?"

"He said there was some kind of problem with the computer system the previous week and some of the client records did not update correctly. He indicted the system had been fixed since then and he would send an updated, correct statement."

"Did he?" asked Bill.

"He did. I received it on Tuesday or Wednesday I believe," said Vallory.

"We got ours on Thursday," Sandra added, "and like yours, the numbers - the rate of return and the balance - seemed to be right in line with where they should be."

"Well here we are," said Sandra as the taxi came to a stop in front of her house.

"This is fine for us too," said Chad to the driver as they all piled out. "It's a short walk from here for us." Vallory and Sandra paid for the taxi and he was off, leaving the four of them outside of Sandra's house in the stillness of the night with the cool desert air and a gentle breeze out of the southwest.

"I think you hit the nail on the head a little earlier, Val when you said this is a little disconcerting," said Chad.

"It may be nothing," offered Bill. "Let's take another look at our statement, make sure it's correct. Unfortunately, tomorrow is Saturday so we may have to wait until Monday to reach out to Carl and see what happened with that check. It is probably just some oversight. Meanwhile, we can go online tonight and transfer some money from our savings account to make sure the mortgage gets paid on time."

"You're probably right, Bill. I've been with Carl and BFSG for a few years now and there has never been a problem, either with my statements or whenever I have requested a withdrawal. There has never been any issues. It isn't like he's a Bernie Madoff or somebody," said Vallory, laughing a little nervously.

"Although I've never met the man, everything I have heard from Chad and others in the group suggests he's a nice guy and a solid financial adviser," said Bill. Chad and Vallory slowly nodded, indicating their agreement.

"Well anyway," Sandra said, "thank you for thinking of us and a wonderful evening."

"Definitely," agreed Vallory.

"You're both very welcome. So what's going on next week for everyone?"

"George and I are traveling to North Carolina to see his sister and I believe that Charles is going to Wisconsin to visit with his daughter."

"Melanie, right?"

"Yep. As for me, I'm having some crown molding and new blinds installed next week so I'll be pretty busy," said Vallory.

"What do you guys think about a dinner party next Saturday then?" asked Sandra.

"Everybody should be back in town. George and I will host."

"Sounds good to us," said Bill, as he looked at Chad and confirmed.

"Good. I'll send out an e-mail to the group and confirm that everyone can make it."

"Sounds good."

"Well, good night, ladies. It's late, I'm tired and I need to get my beauty sleep," said Chad.

There's a joke in there somewhere, thought Vallory.

"Don't even say whatever it is you're probably thinking," warned Chad, giving his friend a knowing smile.

"Moi?" said Vallory, as she gave her friend a sly wink. "Good night, we'll talk to you guys soon."

"Enjoy your trip to North Carolina," Bill encouraged Sandra.

"Will do, Hon."

[4] SUSPICIONS

Monday night. "It will be good to get back to North Carolina to see Barb," mused George, feeling somewhat melancholic. Sandra reminded her husband that they were just there nine months ago to see his sister.

"That's true," he said, "but even though she denies it, I'm convinced her health is deteriorating faster than she is willing to acknowledge."

"If that's true, she probably just doesn't want you to worry. She's been a wonderful big sister to you and I'm just glad we have the means to visit as often as we please or as necessary," said Sandra as they pulled into the Terminal 1 - Economy Parking area at McCarran.

"She has been a great sister. She has always been there for me with a receptive ear, sage advice or quite frankly, a kick in the ass when I needed it. I've been blessed," George said wistfully as he spotted an empty spot and pulled in quickly.

With plenty of time to spare, they made their way to the American Airlines counter at a leisurely pace as those that were in more of a hurry whizzed by them. "There is always so much frenetic energy at airports," Sandra remarked. Arriving at the service counter, they checked their bags and got their boarding passes. Fortunately, with a late departure time, 11:30 p.m., there weren't a lot of people and making their way through the TSA security checkpoint was fairly painless. Within 10 minutes they were seated in the gate area with what looked to be about 25 other travelers.

"I'm going to use the ladies room. Did you want to hit the men's room before we leave?"

"Nope, I believe I'm good to go."

Twenty minutes later the gate agents started the boarding process:

> "Ladies and gentlemen welcome to American Airlines flight number #2364 with service to Miami. We are ready to board our passengers with disabilities, families with small children or those that might require a little extra time boarding the aircraft. Please check your boarding passes as we will be boarding by group numbers. Thank you."

"The last time we were out there you had asked if she had long-term care insurance, correct?"

"I did and she said, yes."

"So how ... "

> "At this time our first class passengers are welcome to board. First class, please."

"So how does that work again? How is the long-term insurance different from regular health insurance?"

"Unlike traditional health insurance, long-term care insurance is designed to cover long-term services and supports which might include things such as personal and custodial care in a number of different settings such as an individual's home, a community organization or other facility. The insurance ... "

> "At this time our first class passengers are welcome to board. First class, please."

"The insurance reimburses policyholders a daily amount, up to a pre-selected limit, for services to assist them with typical daily activities such as bathing, dressing or eating. When buying a policy, an individual can select the range of care options and benefits that allow them to get the services they believe they will require, and perhaps most importantly, where they may need them. Hold on a second, here she goes again."

> "Thank you for your patience ladies and gentlemen. At this time we will continue the boarding process with our Executive Platinum and Platinum Advantage members."

"That sounds like something that will work out well for her, particularly since Edward passed so young, she never remarried and you guys don't really have any other family in the area."

"Yep," George agreed.

> "Thank you for your patience ladies and gentlemen. At this time we'll continue boarding with our Gold Advantage members and active duty military personnel in uniform. Priority Access and Group One may get in line. Thank you."

"How long is the layover in Miami?" Sandra asked.

"Just over three hours," said George as he stood quickly. "We get into Raleigh-Durham at 11:49 tomorrow morning. On second thought, I think I will hit the men's room before we board." Leaving his small carry-on bag with his wife, he raced toward the men's room, two gates down. As he turned into the bathroom, brushing past two teens making hasty exits, he heard their gate agent in the background:

> "Thank you for your patience ladies and gentlemen. At this time we'll continue boarding with groups Two and Three. Groups Two and Three please. Groups Two and Three."

Ten minutes later all passengers had boarded and fifteen minutes after that, right on schedule, they were taxiing down the runway, en route to Miami. "Well, we've got a long night in front of us, Mr. Wright."

"Yes we do, Mrs. Wright." As they reached altitude husband and wife both settled into the flight as they pulled out their noise cancellation headphones and Kindles.

Sandra turned her attention to a crossword puzzle while George picked up where he left off, the second chapter, of *Capital in the Twenty-First Century*. Thomas Piketty's magnum opus on wealth and income disparity in Europe and the United States since the 18th century had touched off quite a firestorm when it was released. George was anxious to see what all the hubbub was about.

Based on what he heard and read so far, those who praised the book, generally more liberally inclined, seemed to focus on four salient points: a society's wealth relative to its annual income will grow - or shrink - to a level equal to its net savings rate divided by its growth rate, time and chance inevitably lead to the concentration of wealth in the hands of a relatively small group of individuals, a society in which the rich have a very high degree of economic and political influence results in a rather unpleasant society and a society in which the wealth-to-annual-income ratio is a very large multiple of the growth rate is one in which control over wealth falls to heirs is even more unpleasant - in many ways - than one dominated by an entrepreneurial rich elite. Conversely, those who are more inclined to conservative ideology tended to argue that inequality is not as bad as Piketty suggests, believe that he is making a case for wealth redistribution - something greatly frowned upon - and the tax-return-based estimates that he has compiled are not without problems. *I look forward to the read*, George thought.

Milwaukee. His old hometown; the place he raised his family and where his daughter remained. He typically visited Melanie a couple times a year, in the spring and fall. Summers in Milwaukee weren't bad but he avoided winters at all costs. He was no fan of the cold and the snow. There was a reason he had retired to the Nevada desert. Spring and fall visits worked out well for both of them. Last spring they had caught a couple Brewer's games and in the past they often managed to catch a Packer's game during his fall visit. Not this year however, as they weren't able to score a couple of tickets. No significant plans this visit; just spend a little time together.

After disembarking from the plane at General Mitchell airport, Charles quickly made his way down to the baggage claim area, secured his bag and headed straight for the car rental counter. While he waited for the agent to finish up the paperwork, he pulled out his phone and fired off a text message: *to Melanie - landed safely on my way to your house see ya tonight.*

As a bank officer and member of M&I Bank's senior management team, Melanie was too busy to break away from work to pick him up. He actually preferred it that way. He was intimately familiar with Milwaukee and he had a key to her condominium so he could let himself in. No need for her to take time away from work to deal with him. He was just fine on his own in his old hometown. Finding his way around his old stomping grounds was not a problem.

Leaving the airport, he made his way north to East Howard Avenue and onto I-94 North. Twenty minutes later he was parked at his daughter's condo on North 17th Street, near Marquette University. Dragging his bag through the front door, he made his way to the guest bedroom and dropped it in the corner. Kicking off his shoes, he figured he would get cleaned up a little, wash his face and hands, and watch a little television for awhile. He never got around to turning the television on. After washing up, he sat down on the edge of bed and laid back to rest his eyes for a minute ... or so he thought. Within two minutes he was fast asleep.

"Dad. Dad. Were you a little sleepy?"

"What? What time is it?"

"It's 5:20 p.m. I just got home. How are you? It's good to see you."

"Hey there, Babe. I must have been more tired than I thought and fell asleep." Rising to his feet, he gave his daughter a hug and a peck on the cheek.

"How was the flight?"

"Uneventful, which is good. How was work today?" he managed after a quick yawn.

"Same thing, uneventful. Are you hungry?"

"Actually, I am. I'm starving. What are we having tonight?"

"To tell you the truth I have been slammed at work all week. I really haven't had a chance to make it to the grocery store. I could go look in the refrigerator, but honestly, it would be a waste of time. Other than some orange juice, mayonnaise, spaghetti sauce, milk that is likely spoiled and a cucumber, not too much going on in there. Want to go get something?"

"Sure. Do you have a taste for anything specifically?"

"Not really. How about you?"

"You know me, I always love Italian. I could probably alternate between Mexican and Italian every day of the week. What was the name of the place we went to the last time I was here? The one over on West Wisconsin Avenue. Was it Saul's or something like that?"

"Pizza place on West Wisconsin?" Melanie mumbled as her brow furrowed. "Oh, you mean Sal's?"

"Yeah, that was it. A calzone sounds good."

"That works for me. Give me a few minutes, I want to get these shoes and bra off and change into some more comfortable clothes."

"Well, that might have been a little too much information, Babe."

The smell of fresh baked bread, the hint of roasted garlic and oregano lingering in the air were absolutely sublime. Reveling in the savory aromas of Italian cuisine, Charles realized he was more hungry than he thought. They grabbed a table and ordered two waters, with lemons, when the waiter came over.

"I assume you're going to order a calzone," said Melanie.

"Yep, I believe so. These may be the best calzones I've ever had."

"Really?" asked his daughter. "Out of all the places you were stationed and had Italian food, these are the best?"

"Yep. I believe so."

"Better than that mom and pop place at Fort Bragg, over by the mall in Fayetteville? Or the one in Martinez, outside Fort Gordon? How about that gasthaus in Landstuhl, Germany?"

"Yep, yep and yep."

"Wow, that says a lot."

"As I remember it, they are that good."

Making his way back to the table, the waiter informed the pair that he was ready to take their order. "Ma'am?"

"I'll try the vegetarian calzone. What exactly does that come with?"

"Our signature red sauce, garlic salt, vegan cheese, black olives, diced onions and sun-dried tomatoes."

"Perfect. That should work."

"And you, sir?"

"I will have a calzone with pepperoni, spicy salami and Canadian bacon."

"Will that be all?"

"Oh, and some extra mozzarella. That should do it," replied Charles. "Thank you."

"So what's going on in your world?" Charles asked his daughter.

"Actually quite a bit."

"Oh really?" said Charles, sitting up a little more upright as the inflection and slight change in the tone of her voice told him that whatever his daughter was about to share was pretty important.

"I found out a couple of days ago but I figured I would wait until you got out here to share ... "

"Is something wrong, Melanie?" Charles asked, a touch of worry creeping into his voice.

"No dad. There is absolutely nothing to worry about. In fact, it's good news. I have been offered a Vice President position."

"Wow! That is quite the news. Congratulations, Melanie. Is the position here in Milwaukee at one of the other branches?"

"No, and that is the one thing giving me pause. The position is in Minnesota at a branch in Brooklyn Park. Ever been to Minnesota?

"I have not."

"I haven't given an answer yet. I'm flying out there next week to check it out."

"What does Doug have to say?"

"Not a lot at this point. He has tried to be supportive but it's tough. He just got a promotion himself, about two months ago, and he is developing deeper roots here. In a nice way, our relationship has gotten more serious which makes it all a lot more complicated."

"I'm sure it does. I know it's somewhat cliché, but perhaps the best way to approach this is to start a list of each of the pros and cons, assigning a certain weight to each. Once you return from Minnesota, finish up the list taking into account your impressions of the Brooklyn Park branch and the opportunities available there, not only at the bank, but in the community as a whole."

"I think you're right, dad. That sounds like a great approach."

"Anything else going on?"

"Yeah, I'm working with our Human Resources department to develop a training program covering 401(k) loans. This has become a priority for corporate so the local leadership is very focused on the success of the program. Once the training is developed and approved by the board, it will be part of the required training regimen for all the Milwaukee area branches."

"What specifically is the training going to cover?"

"Well, actually there will be two parts to it."

"First is the training for management. There have been a lot of questions recently with respect to the conditions surrounding eligible loans. Our HR department has had a difficult time getting managers to understand that generally, the ability of employees to access funds in their 401(k) accounts prior to retirement is restricted. Although some employees find it difficult to accept, they are not able to withdraw funds from their accounts, even in the event of hardship, unless strict conditions are met. One way around this of course, is to allow employees to take out loans against their account balances. However, the loan program must meet several requirements designed to ensure that plan loans do not constitute prohibited transactions that may subject the employee and the employer to an excise tax. Unfortunately, without a 401(k) loan option, many employees would be reluctant to tie up funds that they may need to purchase a car, make a down payment on a home, or to pay for medical care or other large or unexpected expenses. Though a 401(k) loan program provides some benefits, there are some downsides. The plan loans contain hidden costs and pose retirement risks; that leads to the second part of the training, which is geared toward educating employees."

"We're trying to let employees know that while they can take out 401(k) loans, they need to be aware that the amount of the loan may not exceed the lesser of $50,000 or one-half of the present value of the participant's vested benefit; the terms of the loan - except principal residence loans - must be repaid within five years; and the loan must be amortized on a substantially level basis with payments made no less frequently than quarterly. Additionally, employees need to realize that, although loans allow them to avoid the tax penalties typically imposed on in-service withdrawals from a 401(k) plan, plan loans are not without costs."

"Don't I know it," said Charles. "I took out one years ago and was surprised that there was an interest rate associated with the repayment."

"Exactly. Loans invite set-up costs, administrative expenses and transaction fees that are typically deducted from a participant's account. Also, many employees mistakenly believe that they are borrowing money from themselves because the loan reduces their account balance. The reality however, is that the loan is actually being made by the plan and thus must be repaid with interest, even if employment is terminated."

"A significant portion of the training focuses on the fact that even though federal law does not restrict the reasons employees take a loan from a 401(k) plan, the ease with which employees may access their accounts should not encourage employees to treat their account balances as checking accounts. There are serious potential adverse effects of such withdrawals on retirement savings. Specifically, because a participant's account balance must be partially liquidated in order to fund the loan, the income-generating impact of compound interest on the smaller account balance is reduced. As a result, even though the participant is repaying the loan with interest, the repayment terms may not be sufficient to match the lost growth caused by the reduced impact of compound interest on the smaller account balance."

"Interesting. It sounds as if you have a lot on your plate right now."

"I do, but fortunately, I don't really feel overwhelmed. The training is just about complete. I'm just reviewing it now to make sure I haven't left out anything and all the I's are dotted and the T's are crossed."

"Anything new or exciting going on back in the Silver State?"

"Nope. Not too much really."

"Everyone in your little gang is doing alright?"

"Absolutely. Had a nice night out a few days ago with Dave and George. You've met them both."

"I remember. Dave is married to Sandra and George to Mary ... nope, it's the other way around. Correct?"

"Yep. We went out the other night to one of the cigar bars in the area, enjoyed a couple of glasses of scotch, a new hand rolled cigar and good conversation. While we were there, some of the others in the group went to that new Michael Jackson Cirque du Soleil show."

"Sounds cool. What did you guys talk about as you enjoyed your stogies and scotch?"

"Pretty much the same ol' stuff. Who is doing what to whom in the community, the new clubhouse, golfing, investments and retirement income."

"How are you doing anyway?"

"On the investments and retirement income?"

"Yeah."

"My investments are doing well. Heck, I pretty much have more than I need. I suppose there aren't any real issues with BFSG."

"What do you mean, 'no real issues?'"

"When we were out the other night, Dave had asked if George and I were happy with BFSG. George stated that he was happy with the fact that the returns have been very consistent. Rightly so, he noted that is definitely a priority for retirees. At this stage of our lives it is more important to protect our money and ensure that a consistent income stream can be drawn from investments. However, he wasn't ... "

"I have the vegetarian calzone," said the waiter as he slid the plate in front of Melanie, "and one calzone with pepperoni, spicy salami, Canadian bacon and extra mozzarella. Can I get you folks anything else?"

"I don't believe so," Melanie and Charles replied in unison.

"Enjoy."

"Thank you."

"Smells divine," said Melanie.

"However," Charles continued, "he wasn't too happy with some services ... or more accurately, the lack of some services. He correctly noted that you can't manage investment accounts online. The only thing really offered via the BFSG website is the ability to view a listing of their services and contact information. Services such as viewing and downloading statements are not available."

"That does seem odd," agreed Melanie.

"I guess, however, it has never been a huge deal for me. What was a little disconcerting though is the fact that when George got his most recent quarterly statement he noticed that the balance was exactly the same as the previous quarter. While my most recent quarterly statement showed the typical 6% monthly gain ... "

"Six percent?!" Monthly? Are you serious?"

"Yes, 6% monthly is the guaranteed rate of return. While my most recent quarterly statement showed the anticipated gains, I had the same issue that George had with my previous quarterly statement. Like me, George spoke to our advisor, Carl, and he gave us both the exact same explanation. He noted that, 'there was some kind of problem with their computer system the previous week and some of the client records did not update accurately. However, the system had been fixed since then and he would send an updated statement.'"

"I've got to tell ya, dad, something just doesn't sound right. Six percent returns? Monthly? Guaranteed? The inability to manage your account online? While there is no doubt that computer systems experience problems all the time, what are the odds that different clients will experience the exact same issue three months apart?"

"How was the trip?" Barb asked, giving her baby brother and sister-in-law long, soulful hugs as they entered the baggage claim area. It was always great to see the two of them.

"The long layover in Miami sucked, but overall uneventful; therefore, a good trip. How are you? You look great," said George.

"I feel good. Great in fact. Quickly changing the subject, Barb agreed with her brother. "Sometimes uneventful is good. Are you guys hungry? We could stop somewhere and get a bite to eat if you are."

"I could use a bite," said Sandra, turning to her husband. "How about you?"

"Sure, I could stand to eat something."

"You guys have a taste for anything in particular?" asked Barb.

"Nope," said Sandra, answering for the both of them. "It's your town, we'll leave the choice in your very capable hands."

Following lunch at Olive Garden, the threesome loaded themselves back into Barb's VW Touareg and headed to her home. After unpacking their suitcase and settling in their guest room, George and Sandra kicked their shoes off and laid down for what was intended to be a short power nap. Three hours later, Sandra awoke to find her husband sleeping soundly and a quiet house. Awaking her husband from his slumber, she swung her feet off the bed and to the floor. Enjoying the warmth of the thick rug beneath her feet, she extended both arms over her head and enjoyed a good stretch and deep yawn. "On your feet, sleepyhead," she said, encouraging her husband to climb out of bed before he fell back asleep. "What time is it?" George inquired. Focusing her eyes on the small alarm clock on the nightstand, "Just after 4:30," she informed him. "Your sister must be out, it's awfully quiet." As they shuffled about the room and changed into some more comfortable clothing, they heard the familiar sound of the garage door opening. "That must be Barb," George, still half asleep, mumbled to his wife.

Walking downstairs, George made his way through the kitchen just as his sister was walking through the connecting door to the garage with a couple bags of groceries.

"I see you guys have woken up. Get enough rest?"

"Yep. I feel a lot better. I was a lot more tired than I thought. I was mistaken in my belief that I just needed to shut my eyes for a few minutes."

"Can I assume Sandra is up also?"

"She is. She'll probably walk down in a minute. Need help? Any more bags out there?"

"Just three or four more. I thought I'd pick up some groceries for the next few days. If you'll bring them in I'll start putting these away. How does a mixed green salad and grilled salmon sound? I figured we'd go a little lighter on dinner after that heavy pasta for lunch."

"Sounds perfect," answered Sandra who had just come down the stairs and made her way into the kitchen. "Anything I can help you with, Barb?"

"Sure," Barb said, "you can get the salad made up while I prepare the salmon."

After bringing in the last few bags, George opened a bottle of red wine and poured a glass for everyone before moseying into the living room and turning on the television. With his glass of wine in one hand and the remote control in the other he flipped through the stations, ending up on FOX Business Network. Setting the remote control down on the coffee table, he plopped down on the sofa with his glass of wine and fixed his eyes on the television where the host was interviewing the head of a major financial advisory firm. *This should be interesting he thought.*

Host: "For many Americans, it used to be that your employer provided, and managed, your retirement plan."

Guest: "Believe me, that has changed. Now, a lot of the decisions that need to be made with respect to saving, investing and retirement, employees have to make on their own."

Host: "So now the tables have turned. Corporations have stepped back and put the responsibility, along with more of the cost, on the individual. Correct?"

Guest: "You're exactly right. The pension system has changed quite dramatically over the last twenty years or so. People aren't going to have pensions like they used to, where they get a benefit for the rest of their lives after 30 or 40 years of service. Basically, people are going to retire with 401(k) plans, and maybe an IRA, that they've managed themselves."

Host: "It appears as if Generation X, those born roughly between 1965 - 1984, has found itself long on life expectancy and short on savings. Is that pretty accurate?"

Guest: "You're absolutely right. I think this is a crisis in the making. Ten or twelve years from now, as the leading edge of this generation reaches their 60s, and starts retiring, many are simply not going to have enough money to retire comfortably."

Host: "How did we get into this mess?"

Guest: "It's not something that happened overnight. The story slowly unfolded over the course of more than 20 years and the implications are just now starting to come into focus."

Forty minutes later his wife called him into the dining room, they were ready to eat.

"I was just telling your sister about the strange occurrence with our last quarterly statement from BFSG."

"Made even more strange when you consider the same thing happened with Charles three months prior, with the previous quarterly statement," George noted.

"Really?" Sandra asked "I didn't know that."

"That is what Charles said the other night when we were out at the West Wing Cigar Lounge. He said that Carl had noted there was some kind of problem with their computer system the previous week and some of the client records did not update accurately. However, the system had been fixed since then and he would send an updated, correct statement."

"Well that is a little disconcerting," said Sandra. "That is pretty much exactly what he told us … and Val."

"Maybe a little disconcerting, but likely nothing to worry about," said George in a calm, measured tone.

"While I certainly don't want to come across as an alarmist," Barb said, "I'm not so sure there shouldn't be some concern, George. It sounds to me as if this is something you two should look into in greater detail. The issue with statements and the inability to manage accounts online reminds me of that case a couple of years ago with that financial firm in the Midwest, Iowa I think it was."

"What case?" asked George as a quizzical look came across his face.

"The founder, I think his name was Wasenford or Wallendorf, something like that, attempted to commit suicide as the authorities were closing in, preparing to arrest him on suspicion of fraud. Before his failed suicide attempt and subsequent arrest, he had written a confession letter stating that he had been using a scheme that made use of false bank statements to embezzle millions of dollars from customer accounts over a period of about 20 years or something like that."

"Twenty years?" asked Sandra, shocked.

"Yep. If I remember correctly, the authorities discovered a $200 million shortfall in customer funds. Later, it came out that he had stolen the money during that period using little more than Photoshop and inkjet printers to fabricate fake bank statements and dupe regulators."

Thursday night. Henderson, Nevada. Parked a quarter of a block down and across the street, Morrison eased back in his seat as his eyes darted back and forth between the second floor, where his office was located, and the parking lot where Darlene's car was parked in its usual spot, the middle of the parking lot underneath the one functioning streetlight. She liked to be as near as possible to the one light source as she occasionally worked late. However, on most nights she left promptly at 5:30. It was nearly 5:30 now and he suspected she would be walking out any moment. In at 8:30 a.m. and out at 5:30 p.m. every day. His administrative assistant was a model of consistent behavior. Sure enough, two minutes later he saw her descending the stairs. Two minutes after that, she pulled out of the lot and headed east on Flamingo Road. He wasn't concerned with anyone else being in the office, after all, only the two of them remained as he had been forced to lay-off the six analysts that were on his staff, over the period of nine months, as the economy dragged along. However, he figured he would wait another hour or so and let it get darker. Moreover, he didn't want to take a chance that she would return to the office for some reason; perhaps to send an email she had neglected to send earlier or grab some paperwork she had forgotten.

An hour later, when it was sufficiently dark and the odds that Darlene would return had greatly diminished, he made his way down the block, turned into the parking lot Darlene had left an hour ago, but unlike his administrative assistant, chose a spot as far as possible from the single streetlight. The darker, the better. Getting out of his car, he silently ascended the exterior stairs and swiftly made his way to his office. Opening the door, he reached out, flicked the light switch on and walked over to his desk. Sitting down, he reached into the drawer and pulled out the letters from Bank of the West. He had already looked them over multiple times, and after a few minutes re-reading them, he determined no new information was forthcoming; and although he had borrowed - *which prosecutors would likely define as stealing*, he thought to himself - money from client accounts in the past, perhaps two times in the last year, to meet capital requirements, he had determined that was no longer an option. He would have to find another way to meet his obligation on the $3 million loan.

In the meantime, he had to be prepared in case things went south. He didn't want to be the next Bernie Madoff or Allen Stanford, prominent financiers that found themselves in jail after a fraud was discovered. He would do everything in his power to get his client's accounts right and get this ship turned around. However, if he couldn't, he needed an exit plan. Going to prison was absolutely not an option. He was too old to fight and he abhorred the thought of his ass being used as a playground. After fifteen minutes of sitting alone in the quiet office, it was clear to him that nothing else could be accomplished here and he decided it was time to go. Halfway to the door, he changed his mind and headed back to the desk. Sitting down, he tore a piece of paper out of the notebook on his desktop and penned a quick note to Darlene; and dropped it off on her desk on his way out. Just as quickly as he had ascended the stairs 20 minutes earlier, he descended them now and walked quickly to his car. Exiting the lot, he disappeared into the darkness.

Friday morning. "Do you want to just drive over to his office?" Bill asked.

"Maybe," Chad answered. Although I wasn't able to reach him yesterday, I did leave a message. It's just after 9:00 a.m. now, he should be in his office by now. Maybe he was ill or something yesterday and took the day off."

"Possible," Bill said, "but don't you think his assistant, Darlene, would have been there even if he was out sick?"

"True," Chad agreed. "Hell, let me try his office again." Almost immediately, Chad pulled the phone away from his ear, hung up and dialed again. "Hold on a minute, I think I fat fingered it and dialed the wrong number." Poking away at the phone's keypad with a lone forefinger, Chad slowly and deliberately punched in the numbers a second time. Again, almost immediately, he pulled the phone away from his ear. Looking as white as a ghost, he sat – or more accurately – fell back into the couch.

"What's wrong?" Did it just go to voicemail again?" asked Bill.

"No," Chad managed to mumble, "the number has been disconnected."

"Disconnected? What do you mean disconnected."

"I don't know how else to put it, Bill. The BFSG office phone number has been disconnected."

"Yep. Houston, I think we may have a problem," groaned Bill.

[5] ANSWERS

Saturday night. The group had gathered at George and Sandra's home. Little did any of them imagine, a week ago, when this little dinner party was planned, that they would be discussing a growing concern that something had happened to Carl Morrison, and more importantly, their money. An ad hoc meeting was now taking place before dinner. While the degree to which they were each concerned varied, conversations among themselves and with family members had convinced them all that something probably was not right. Something definitely was not quite right. Their concerns were reinforced by three factors. First, those who tried to contact Carl were left slack-jawed when they were consistently greeted with a voicemail message and then most recently, like Chad, the familiar tone of a disconnected telephone line when they called his office ... the former BFSG office? Second, the bounced check Carl had given Chad and Bill. And third, through a chance encounter with Darlene, Morrison's personal assistance, yesterday at the Trader Joe's on Green Valley Parkway, Charles had become absolutely convinced they had a serious problem.

Standing in George and Sandra's living room, Charles explained how he had run into Darlene, quite literally, as he turned into the chips and snack foods aisle and she had run over his left foot with her shopping cart. Not recognizing him at first, she simply apologized. However, the moment the recognition set in, her face became ashen and she attempted to quickly excuse herself. Moving quickly to his left, he had impeded her movement and asked how she was.

"I'm well, Mr. Bingman. Other than being a little overwhelmed at work, things are well," she had responded.

"At work?" he had challenged her. He noted that he had found that interesting considering he had been unable to reach Carl at the office. In fact, every time he called all he got was the voicemail.

"That's odd," Darlene offered.

"Yes it is," he had said, "very odd." Again, Darlene attempted to angle her cart to move forward, only to be thwarted by him.

"Can you tell me what's going on, Darlene?" he had asked with some sternness.

Her reply was a weak and not very believable, "I'm not sure what you mean and I'm really in a hurry, Mr. Bingman. Perhaps if you just call the office tomorrow," she had said as she pushed her cart forward more forcefully.

He had casually reminded her that all he got was a voicemail message when he called. Trying to be as direct as possible, he had asked, "are you saying the Carl will be in the office tomorrow?" Ignoring the question, she instead forcefully angled her cart to extricate herself from her position. He had started to impede her movement a third time; however, traffic had started to build behind her, their conversation had grown more loud and other shoppers were starting to take notice. Using his best judgment, he let her pass. As she moved passed him, he had looked her squarely in the eye and informed her, "when you see Carl, let him know we need to talk ... and we need to talk soon."

It probably was no surprise that Charles, a retired Army Master Sergeant and an experienced leader, had taken charge of the meeting. The constant redirects to voicemail was bad enough and a little disconcerting. The fact that the BFSG phone was now disconnected, as discovered by Chad, was beyond disconcerting and downright troubling. As his friends continued to give him their full attention, he laid things out as he saw them.

"The way I see it, we have three choices," he started, with an air of authority. "One, we do nothing and hope we're wrong. Cross our fingers and just hope that the incorrect statements, the bounced check and the disconnected phone are just odd occurrences and not indicative of a significant problem. Two, we go to the authorities with what we know, hope it's enough to arrest him and pray our money isn't in some offshore account ... one we, or the authorities, will never be able to get to. Or three, we take matters into our own hands and take our money back. The problem with number one is if we're wrong, and he is stealing our money, we'll all be broke before long. Nothing. Nada. We can all forget those comfortable retirements we envisioned. The problem with number two is that if we go to the authorities and they arrest him; and the money is in some offshore bank in the Caribbean, or some other God awful location with strict bank privacy laws, we'll never get it back. It will be lost down there forever. And the prob ... " Charles paused as Bill cleared his throat.

"The problem as I see it with number three is that none of us are ninjas," said Bill, interrupting him. "How do we go about taking our money back? What are we going to do, scale the exterior of the office building at 2 a.m. and break into his offices ... or if we do find out where the money is being kept, what are we going to do, break into a bank? Who are we, Ocean's Eight?"

"Well, damn it! That's the reason we're here, Bill, to review all of our options, discuss various courses of action, agree on the best one and act," said Charles, his voice reaching a slow crescendo. They should have started this meeting before Bill got a couple of glasses of wine in him and fancied himself a comedian. Bill's ninja and Ocean's Eight references had elicited a few chuckles and Charles was already frustrated with the group. After everyone had settled down a little, Charles started again. "Now look, here is the bottom line, and you all know it. Options one and two are shit. Pure rhinoceros feces. Our best chance ... "

"Scat."

"What's that, Val?"

"I believe rhinoceros poop is called scat," replied Vallory.

Doing his best to remain calm, Charles continued. "As I was saying - before our friend Bill shared his thoughts on ancient covert agents in feudal Japan and Val provided a *Mutual of Omaha* teaching moment - our best bet for getting our money back, whatever may be left, is to take it back. Do it ourselves and do it soon before Morrison flees the country, spends it all or both."

Charles reminded them that combined, Morrison managed over $3.75 million of their money. "Whatever we do, we need to do it as a group. Now you all know where I stand. Let's quit fartin' around and take the vote. By a show of hands, how many choose option one?" One hand shot up. "How many choose option two?" Two hands shot up. "How many choose option three?" Another two hands. "Counting myself, that makes three for option three."

"Although Mary and I don't have any money with BFSG, three sounds like the best choice to me," said Dave. Mary nodded in agreement.

"It looks like we have a choice," said Charles. "Remember, friends, this is Vegas, and whatever is decided in this room, and happens going forward, stays between us. Now let's develop a plan for getting our money back."

"So where do we start?" Chad asked, posing the question to the group. No one replied. "Does anyone know anything about Morrison outside of his role at BFSG?" asked Bill.

"I believe he mentioned something about scuba diving ... or maybe it was snorkeling," said Sandra. "I suppose that probably isn't too helpful."

"I've heard him mention hiking the Frenchman Mountain Summits and Echo Canyon. Unfortunately, like the snorkeling, I'm not sure how helpful that is." A long silence followed. The group only sat there and looked at each other. "I've never met or spoken to the man; I really don't know anything about him outside of what Chad has told me," said Bill as he looked over at his partner.

"How about a home address? A home phone number?" Nothing from the group. Finally, after a long silence ...

"Darlene."

"What's that, Sandra?" asked Charles.

"It seems to me that the best place for us to start is to talk with Darlene, his administrative assistant. It appears as if we won't be able to contact him at the office and it looks like we don't have a way to contact him at his home. True?" After no one responded, she continued. "Moreover, while it is likely that he assumes some of his clients are growing suspicious, he probably figures he has some time to act. If we confront him, he will be more inclined to act quickly to hide, or spend, the money. It seems to me our best bet is to make contact with Darlene as soon as possible and see what she knows."

"That sound reasonable to me," offered Vallory.

"Yep," mumbled Chad, nodding his head.

"That does sound reasonable," agreed Mary, "but we don't where she lives either."

"True," agreed Sandra. "However, we know where she shops."

Monday afternoon. Sitting in the Trader Joe's parking lot, Charles and George waited. The group had started surveilling for Darlene yesterday. Vallory had taken a four hour shift yesterday morning while Chad and Bill had put in six hours in the afternoon. No luck yesterday, and so far, no luck today. An hour after their arrival they sat in silence and waited. Nothing. "Well, this is about the time I saw her the other day," said Charles, breaking the silence ... just after breaking wind.

"Good night, Charles!" George said as he lowered his previously cracked window all the way. "You need to check your diet, my friend. Hopefully she's a creature of habit," George finally offered. "What's your guess on the extent of the damage?"

"Carl and BFSG?"

"Yeah. Sandra has asked and I don't have a good answer for her. If it's bad, real bad, I take some comfort in the fact that we have passive income, via our pensions, and we're not wholly reliant on portfolio income, the money we had with BFSG."

"I know what you mean. I'm fortunate that I have my pension from the Army and some money in an IRA, with a different financial services company of course. I'm not completely reliant on the money I have with BFSG. However, I have been kicking myself in the ass the last few days."

"Why is that?"

"While I have some other sources of income, the majority of my money is with BFSG and my overall portfolio is not as diversified as it should be, which is kind of funny."

"Funny? Funny in what way?"

"I had a conversation with Dave and Mary about four months ago where I extolled the virtues of diversification. I gave them the entire rundown. Mary had made a comment suggesting that it wasn't that important to maintain different types of investments ... "

"You're talking about splitting investments between different asset classes such as stocks, fixed income - such as bonds or certificates of deposit - and cash, correct?" said George, interrupting Charles.

"Yes, however, the best diversification goes beyond the three most well known asset classes and encompasses the idea that investments should not be concentrated in one company, country or industry."

"Makes sense."

"So when I spoke with Mary I reminded her that the rationale for mixing a wide variety of investments within a portfolio was that it served as an important risk management technique; that studies have shown that a portfolio of different kinds of investments will, on average, yield higher returns and pose a lower risk than any individual investment found within the portfolio. In a line that probably sounded like it came straight from a personal finance pamphlet, I told her that diversification strives to smooth out unsystematic risk events in a portfolio so that the positive performance of some investments will counterbalance the negative performance of others."

"Sounds reasonable to me. It sounds like good guidance."

"It is. The problem is that I didn't practice what I was preaching like I should have been. I had been meaning to pull some money from BFSG with their limited selections, and get more exposure to international investments. Although they don't have money with BFSG, I hope Dave and Mary took my guidance to heart, the guidance I failed to follow myself. As far as the damage, I have no idea. That's why it's important to gather as much information as possible, as soon as possible, and determine if there is a way to salvage whatever remains. Using Darlene as the conduit to more information is probably the way to go."

"I guess we'll see," said George, his voice trailing off as he stared out the window at the overcast, darkening sky. As the temperature slowly dropped, the friends sat in near silence, listening to the smooth jazz of KUNV, 91.5 FM, playing low in the background.

Two hours later, just as Charles stepped out of the car for a bathroom break, George called out, "Hey isn't that her?" Stopping himself in mid-stride and looking toward the entrance, Charles replied, "Where? I don't see her."

"Just exited. Red blouse and jeans. Isn't that her?" George insisted.

"What the hell! I don't see her."

"Red blouse," repeated George. "The only one in a red blouse."

"I'll be damned. Yep, it is," Charles confirmed after a brief moment. "How did we miss her going in? I'll be damned!"

"I don't know, but we've got her in our sights now."

"I guess the bathroom will have to wait," said Charles, jumping back into the car.

The next part of their plan was pretty straight forward. Follow Darlene. Follow her all the way home and confront her with the information they had and compel her to reveal what was going on with Carlton Morrison and BFSG.

"Here we go," said Charles as he started the car and pulled out of the parking lot.

"Yep, here we go," echoed George.

After nearly an hour and a half of following her around, with stops at four different stores, George was growing tired and frustrated. "How much longer are we going to follow her? Why don't we just confront her at the next store she stops at?"

"As we discussed, we follow her to her home. It might prove beneficial later to know exactly where she lives, and quite frankly, there is the intimidation factor."

"The intimidation factor?"

"It is much more disconcerting and unnerving if someone confronts you in front of your home, the place you associate with safety and security, vice some retail store in the public square. Be patient, George, my guess is she'll be heading home soon. She can't shop forever."

"I'm not so sure. There are times when Sandra seems to get more energized the longer she's out shopping. There have been a number of times when I thought she couldn't possibly want to hit one more store only to be disappointed when we jumped in the car and she informed me, 'just one more stop.'"

"I bet."

Twenty minutes later, Darlene turned off Goldhill Road onto Edgemont Drive, into a residential area. "Here we go," mumbled Charles. She's finally heading home is my guess."

"It's about time!" declared George. As they drove slowly down Edgemont, the garage door of a tan house with dark blue trim, three houses up on the left, started to rise.

"This must be the place," said Charles.

"Indeed. Yes indeed," agreed George. As Darlene pulled into the garage, Charles quickly brought his car to a stop in front of the house next door and both men jumped out and raced toward the open doorway.

As her car door closed behind her, Darlene took the five steps toward the door which lead to her kitchen and reached for the garage door button.

"Darlene!" Charles called out loudly. Startled, Darlene froze in place for a moment as the two men walked into her garage. After a brief moment she was able to compose herself. "Mr. Bingman and Mr. Wright. What are you two doing here!?"

"I think you know why we're here," George answered immediately and firmly.

"This is my home. We should really be doing this at the office. Whatever this is!"

"Oh really?" Charles asked, "and if went by the office, what answers could we possibly have answered? Would we find Carl there?"

Ignoring the questions, Darlene simply stated, "this is highly inappropriate. I'm going to have to ask you gentlemen to leave or I will be forced to call the police."

Sensing this for what it was, Charles called the bluff. "Perhaps that's a good idea, Darlene, why don't you call the police. I believe the authorities would be very interested in hearing about what has been going on at BFSG, interested to hear about what you and Morrison have been up to."

"I haven't been up to anything!" she quickly protested.

"Well then," Charles said, "it only stands to reason that if you haven't personally been involved in anything, you shouldn't have a problem talking to us. Wouldn't you agree?" Again, Darlene simply ignored the question that had been lobbed at her.

"What is going on at BFSG?" George demanded. "You can either tell us or talk to the police and the Nevada Financial Institutions Division!"

"Settle down a little, George. Let's all remain calm," Charles encouraged his friend in a measured tone. "Let's give Darlene a moment to think about the potential implications of involving the authorities."

Watching Darlene, George could see the wheels spinning as she considered the options available to her. After what seemed like five minutes, and multiple occasions when it looked like she would say something, only to fall silent, she finally spoke. "I knew it would come to this. I just knew it."

"Look, Darlene," Charles said, "we don't want any trouble and if I had to guess, I would say you aren't involved in whatever Carl is up to. However, we have strong reason to believe something is going on - what, we don't know - and if we don't act quickly, we, and some of our friends, could face financial ruin. Like I said, we really don't want any trouble but we are going to leave here with answers or involve the authorities immediately and let the chips fall where they may. I would encourage you to give some serious thought to what happens next. What's it going to be? The choice is yours."

With a look of resignation, Darlene extended an invitation for George and Charles to follow her. "Come on in, gentlemen. My husband won't be home for another two hours or so and we can talk in the kitchen. Do you mind helping me with some of these bags?"

"Not a problem," answered Charles. "After the fright we gave you it is probably the least we could do. With all the bags in hand between the three of them, Darlene led Charles and George through the garage door and into the kitchen; and indicated they could set the bags on the kitchen counter. She then motioned for them to have a seat at the dining room table which was located just off the kitchen. "Coffee?" she asked.

"Yes please," replied Charles.

"No thank you. Just some water for me please," said George.

"Coming right up, gentlemen. Just give me a moment to get settled." Setting her two bags on the kitchen counter, she made her way to the living room where she kicked off her shoes and dropped her purse on the sofa.

Walking back through the dining room to the kitchen, she filled the coffee maker with four cups of water. Next, she added two heaping scoops of Yuban Organic Dark Roast, her current favorite. Turning the coffee pot on, she grabbed her mug, adding one teaspoon of sugar and one tablespoon of hazelnut flavored cream. "How do you like your coffee, Mr. Bingman?" she called out.

"Just a little cream please and it's just Charles. Thank you."

"Hazelnut, Irish cream or do you prefer regular cream?"

"The hazelnut is good. Thank you ... actually, I think I'll go with the Irish cream." Reaching into the cupboard, Darlene grabbed a second mug and a glass. After pouring a little Irish cream in the mug she walked over to the refrigerator where she filled the glass at the water dispenser. Making her way to the dining room, she set the glass of water down in front of George before taking a seat at the table, joining her guests.

"Wow. Where to start," said Charles. "As I believe you know, Darlene, among our group of friends, most of us have money, significant amounts of money in fact, invested with Carl and BFSG. Things have happened recently which suggests all is not well with our money. A couple of examples. First, some of us - myself, George here and his wife Sandra and Vallory Jackson - have received quarterly statements that indicated balances that were exactly the same as the previous quarter."

"I don't have anything to do with the quarterly or annual statements," she quickly interjected.

"I'm not suggesting you do. Please, just hear me out. As I was saying, some in our group of friends were surprised to find that their most recent quarterly statements indicated balances that were exactly the same as the previous quarter. More specifically, I had that experience last quarter while George, Sandra and Vallory experienced the same thing this most recent quarter. The most perplexing thing about the experience was that Carl fed the exact same story to each of us. He claimed that there was some kind of problem with your computer system the previous week and some of the client records did not update accurately. However, the system had been fixed since then and he would go ahead and send an updated, correct statement. Now what are the odds that statements sent to different clients, during different quarters, would reflect the same error and could be attributed to the same issue?" Charles asked rhetorically.

"Just one moment," Darlene said as she excused herself, "I believe the coffee is just about ready." Standing by the counter as the coffee finished brewing, Darlene patiently waited. The moment it finished, she grabbed the coffee pot, filled both mugs on the counter and then made her way back to the dining room table with mugs in hand. "Just a little Irish cream," she noted as she extended the first mug to Charles. Noticing that his glass was empty, she offered to get George some more water.

"No thank you," he said. Once she was seated, Charles continued. "Second, William - Bill - Dreyer and Chad Richardson, I believe you know them both ... "

"I do, although I have never met Mr. Dreyer, only spoken to him on the phone. Also, I wanted to tell you that I don't recall any issues with the computers at work, either three months ago, when the last group of quarterly statements went out, or more recently."

"Fair enough," said Charles.

"Bill and Chad received a check from BFSG that bounced," Charles continued. "As you can probably imagine, it is quite disconcerting to receive a check from your financial services company that bounces."

"I imagine that would be troubling."

"Naturally, Bill and Chad attempted to reach out to Carl to find out if there was a problem. Let me restate that. Obviously there's a problem. They called to find out the nature of the problem. Unfortunately, they were not able to reach him. In fact, that is what bring us here today. No one has been able to reach Carl for the last few days. As I indicated when I ran into you at Trader Joe's, every indication is that there is some ongoing issue with the phone system over at BFSG. So, Darlene, as you might imagine, our small group of friends is quite nervous and we are determined to get some answers to our questions. Namely, where is Carl and what is the status of our accounts? What is going on with our money?"

"That certainly is a lot to digest," Darlene began. "The truth is that I don't know the status of your money; and I just found out last Friday that the office phone had been disconnected. It appears Mr. Morrison failed to pay the phone bill. He alone has access to the client accounts and he typically takes care of rent on the office and all of the utilities. My primary responsibilities as an administrative assistant to Mr. Morrison include scheduling appointments, drafting letters and filing paperwork, things along those lines. The ability to view and print copies of statements was the extent of my capabilities with respect to client accounts. As to the question, 'where is Mr. Morrison?' I honestly do not know. I last saw him about a week ago. In hindsight, he had been acting somewhat strangely the last few months. However, I can't point to anything that he said or did specifically that would raise any red flags. Something just wasn't right. The last time I spoke with him he indicated he was going to take a few days off and visit his son in Texas, and return to the office on Thursday."

"I assume this was last Thursday?" Charles asked.

"Yes, last Thursday. I first suspected that something was wrong when he didn't return to the office by noon Thursday and whenever I tried to reach him on his cell phone, or at home, they both went to voicemail. I had told my husband on Thursday night that if Mr. Morrison was not in the office on Friday when I went in, I was going to report him as missing. As I'm sure you are aware, his wife passed a few years ago and he doesn't have any family in the area. He wasn't in the office when I arrived on Friday; however, it was clear that he had been there."

"How do you know that?" asked George.

"The door to his office, which I keep locked when he is not there, was closed but unlocked and a couple of his desk drawers were slightly open. His drawers are always closed and typically locked when he is not around."

"Is it possible there was some type of foul play?" asked Charles.

"That is what I thought initially; however, nothing else in the office was disturbed and he had left a note on my desk."

"What did the note say?" asked George.

"I still have it."

Excusing herself from the table, Darlene disappeared around the corner. Waiting until she was gone and assuming she was out of earshot, George lowered his voice and asked Charles, "so what do you think? Do you believe she is telling the truth?"

"Of course she could just be a good liar, but my guess is that yeah, she's telling the truth." Returning two minutes later with a piece of paper in hand, Darlene placed it on the table in front of Charles and George.

Darlene,

Sorry I haven't been in touch. Things are fine, it's just that I have been very busy lately. I'm going to take a few more days off and spend some time with my son and his family. I should be back in the office on Monday.

~~Mr. Mor~~ Carl

"Well today is Tuesday," Charles said, "I assume it's safe to say you still haven't heard anything from him."

"That's true. I haven't heard anything from him. When he didn't show up I looked for, and found, a phone number for his son. I met him when he came out for his mother's funeral service. In fact, I just called him this morning."

"Great," said George.

"Not really," replied Darlene." I did speak to his son but according to him, he hasn't spoken to his father in at least four months."

Wednesday night. The group gathered at Dave and Mary's place.

"Well, here ... " Charles started to say.

"Sorry, Charles," said Mary, interrupting him. "Before we get started I just wanted to let everyone know that I ordered some pizzas from Papa Murphy's. I hope that works for everyone."

"What did you order?" asked Bill.

"Three larges. A gourmet vegetarian, a spicy fennel sausage and an herb chicken Mediterranean."

"Works for me," said Bill. The rest of the group agreed that the selections were acceptable.

"Well here is what we found out," said Charles, starting again. "He's gone, Morrison has disappeared," Charles informed his friends. We spoke for quite awhile with Darlene, his administrative assistant, and every indication is that Carlton Morrison III has disappeared."

"What exactly did she have to say?" asked Vallory.

"She said she didn't know what was going on with our accounts or the current status of our money."

"Do you believe her?" asked Sandra.

"I do," answered George. As angry as I was and as much as I was hoping she could shed more light, I believe she was telling the truth. I believe the reality is that in her role as an administrative assistant to Morrison her access and knowledge of our accounts is minimal."

"Agreed," said Charles. "George is right. Darlene said that the last time she saw him was about a week ago. At that time he indicated he was going to take a few days off and visit his son in Texas and that he would be back in the office on Thursday."

"Just this last Thursday?" asked Chad.

"Yep, last Thursday."

"When he didn't return to the office by noon Thursday and she couldn't reach Morrison by phone, Darlene decided that if he didn't show up by Friday she was going to report him to the police as missing."

"Did he make it in by Friday?" asked Bill.

"Nope," replied George. "However, he did leave a note. Must have left it sometime Thursday night."

"A note?" asked Vallory. "What the hell did it say?"

"Basically that he was sorry that he had not been in, he was busy ... "

"Busy doing what?"

"I don't really know, Val," offered Charles. "However, the note did say that he was going to spend a few more days with his son in Texas and he would back in the office on Monday."

"As we all know," George said, "he never showed up."

"And this is the kicker," added Charles. According to Darlene, she managed to find a phone number for Morrison's son and she called. However, according to the son, he had not spoken to his father in at least four months. Needless to say, George and I were both momentarily stunned."

"That's it, we're screwed!" proclaimed Chad, throwing up his hands.

"I don't believe so," said Charles.

"Why is that?" asked Sandra.

"As I said, George and I were momentarily stunned after the bombshell about Morrison's son not hearing from him for at least four months. However, after we recovered, we spoke for about another half hour and Darlene shared some interesting information. She noted that she has seen correspondence between Morrison and the firm's banks which indicate that he is having some liquidity issues. Although she doesn't have access to the firm's accounts, nor ours as I noted before, her best guess is that he has been pilfering money from client accounts to meet his other financial obligations. But the good thing - to whatever extent that is possible - is that she hasn't seen any indication that he was using our money to support some lavish new lifestyle; no new cars, houses or boats, nothing like that."

"Quite frankly, that gives me very little comfort," scoffed Chad.

"So what the hell does it all mean?" asked Vallory.

"As I said, in speaking face to face with Darlene, I believe she is telling the truth and that her access to account information is limited. With respect to her hypothesis of what is going on with Morrison, it sounds reasonable. When we spoke to her she had also mentioned that Morrison had been acting somewhat strange the last few months. She couldn't quite put her finger on it but something hasn't been right. It's possible that the reason we got the odd statements is because they were fabricated to hide the real account balances and there were oversights as he was fabricating them. My guess, or perhaps more accurately, my hope, is that he was skimming some money off of each of our - and other client - accounts to meet some other obligations and not to outright steal from us and fund some lavish lifestyle."

"I agree with Chad," said Bill. "That's not exactly comforting."

"No it isn't," agreed Charles. "Although, it really does give me a little bit hope. Helping yourself to someone else's money is stealing regardless of how someone might try to spin it. However, it could be worse. Hopefully what that means is that while our account balances are less than what they should be, or what we thought they were, we haven't been wiped out. Not yet anyway."

"Now that we have had a chance to speak with Darlene, and gather more information, it seems to me that the same options we considered the other night when we first talked about this are still the options available to us. We do nothing and hope we're wrong; keep our fingers crossed and hope that he will just mosey back from wherever he is and our money is just fine. We could go to the authorities with a little more information than we had a few days ago; however, at this point there doesn't seem to be anything that positively points to criminal activity. Additionally, as we said before, if he is detained, arrested or whatever, it makes getting access to our money that much more difficult, or impossible, if he has it off-shore or something. The third option, as we determined last time, is that we take matters into our own hands and take our money back."

"It seems to me that number three is still our best option," proclaimed Vallory.

Sandra, George, Chad and Bill each chimed in with their agreements that number three was still the best option.

"It seems to me that number three is still the best option and of course, we will help any way we can," offered Dave.

"Absolutely," said Mary, as she stood next to her husband, nodding.

"I'm going to head out and get those pizzas," Dave informed the group.

"Need some money?" two or three voices called out.

"Nope. I've got this. I'll be back shortly."

"So what's the next step?" Vallory asked of no one in particular. The question just hung there in the air for awhile until finally, Charles spoke up.

"Well, while we don't know exactly where he is, we can assume there is a fair chance he is still in the area considering he left that note just a few days ago. However, if he has been committing fraud and larceny, which appears to be the case, I think it is reasonable to assume he won't be around long. Also, we have to consider that it is very unlikely that we are his only potential victims. There has to be other clients out there that are asking some of these same questions and probably considering going to the authorities soon, real soon. Anything we do needs to happen quickly."

"So, the question becomes, what is he likely to do?" suggested Sandra.

"If we can figure that out, perhaps we stand a chance of getting out in front of him and getting our money back," reasoned Chad.

"If I was in his shoes, I would be looking at two possible options at this point. My first option would be to find the money to make my clients whole, maybe close some huge deal. If I did, I would just dismiss any questions about the statements, bounced checks and other questionable happenings as just a hiccup, and basically continue on as if nothing was ever wrong. If I was not able to do that within a very short period of time, I might just take all the money I could get my hands on and make a run for the border; go somewhere that does not have an extradition treaty with the United States," said Vallory.

"I'm inclined to agree with you Vallory," offered Charles.

"Yep, agreed," said George. "As dramatic as it sounds, financial fraud is more common than people think and people have been known to take drastic measures when they felt the walls closing in; when they felt the pressures of what they had done were overwhelming."

"Any chance we could get into his office ... without getting a crash course in commando operations, scaling any walls or using dynamite in some way?" Bill asked. That got a little chuckle out of the group.

"Maybe," Charles said. "Apparently Darlene has about $55,000 invested with Morrison and based on his strange behavior and our recent conversation, she is starting to believe she may not see it again. She gave me her phone number and indicated that she would be willing to help if she could. Why? What do you have in mind? Darlene didn't report seeing anything out of the ordinary in the office and I'm not sure what other information we could recover there."

"What about his computer? There might be some information or clues there that we could use," Bill suggested. "In this electronic information age, we are just as likely to find something useful on a computer's hard drive as we would find on filed paperwork."

"Anybody here ever hacked into a computer?" Chad asked. The friends simply looked at each other. "I guess that would be a no," Chad finally mumbled.

After a long silence, Vallory spoke up. "What about your nephew, Mary? isn't he some kind of computer guru?"

"He's a software engineer. He writes the code for a lot of computer games and he knows a lot about computer networks ... "

"That's why I asked, I remember you mentioned that he had fixed some issue on your home computer and set up your Wi-Fi network for you."

"But I don't know if he could, or would, hack into a computer. But hell, I can certainly ask."

"That sounds good," George said, "but we have to get into the office first."

"I'm already on it," said Charles as he pecked away at the keyboard on his phone's screen: *to Darlene - can you get us into the BFSG office? Charles Bingman.*

"And I'm on it," said Mary, grabbing her phone and opening the texting app: *to Paul - give me a call when you have a chance please.*

Twelve minutes later, Dave returned with the pizzas which were promptly grabbed by Mary and thrown into the preheated double ovens. "What did I miss?" he asked.

"We determined that Morrison is likely looking to score a huge deal, putting him into a position to make clients whole, and if he can't do that relatively soon, we believe there is a decent chance he'll bolt for the border," said Sandra.

"Charles has reached out Darlene, who had offered to help more if she could, to see if she can get us into the BFSG office; and I have reached out to Paul ... "

"Your nephew Paul?"

"Yes. I have reached out to Paul to see if he is willing to help us out by getting into Morrison's computer and seeing what information we can recover from that."

"By 'getting into' I assume you mean hack?"

"Yep."

"Here we go," said Charles. "Just got a reply from Darlene. She says she can do that."

"Great!" exclaimed Vallory.

"Any reply from Paul?" asked Dave.

"Nothing yet," replied Mary. "If I don't hear from him tonight I'm sure he'll call tomorrow."

Eighteen minutes later, Mary informed the group that it was time to eat. "It looks like those pizzas are just about finished. Help yourself to something to drink. Everyone knows where the glassware is. We've got water, some juice, soft drinks, beer and some red wine." As the friends enjoyed their pizza, beverages and conversation, the prospect of facing financial ruin was temporarily forgotten.

As the last few slices of pizza disappeared, Sandra addressed the group. "Vallory and I have a tee time of 7:30 tomorrow morning over on the Concord course, anyone care to join us?"

"Did you already make it for a foursome?" asked Bill.

"We did," replied Vallory. "We assumed we could find two among you six to drag out there with us."

"What do you think, Chad?"

"Hell, why not. I'm truly a hack but I need to get in a good walk and I have nothing else going on tomorrow morning. What was the tee time again?"

"The tee time is 7:30 a.m., my friend."

"Sounds good."

"Perfect," said Sandra, just as her phone rang. "It's Paul. Excuse me." Stepping out of the dining room, which had gotten loud with multiple, animated conversations, she took the phone call from her nephew.

Five minutes later Sandra reappeared. "Great news. Paul says he'll help us out. Do we know a day and time yet?"

"I say we go for it tomorrow night; the sooner the better. I will confirm a time with Darlene. I suppose three people should go. I can search the office with Darlene while Paul is doing his thing on the computer and then it probably wouldn't hurt to have someone posted outside just to keep an eye on things. Any volunteers?"

"I'm game," volunteered Vallory.

"That should work out well, Vallory. Do you mind driving your SUV? I think it makes more sense to pick up everyone in one vehicle instead of trying to coordinate a time for everyone to meet there in two or three different vehicles."

"Makes sense to me," said Vallory. I don't mind and my SUV can easily, and comfortably, seat five."

"I'll coordinate with Darlene to pick her up and Mary, I assume you can coordinate with your nephew?"

"Absolutely. I can get you his address, just let me know what time to tell him to be ready. Should I instruct him to wear black clothes?"

"That probably won't be necessary ... " Charles started to say. "Actually, on second thought, it probably wouldn't hurt for everyone to wear dark clothing. Since we will be with Darlene, it's not like we're breaking in ... technically anyway. However, I suppose it probably wouldn't hurt to be inconspicuous and do whatever is necessary to draw as little attention as possible to ourselves."

[6] DISCOVERY

Thursday morning. "Nervous about tonight?" Sandra asked Vallory as they made their way down the 18th fairway with Bill and Chad right behind them in their cart. They had largely avoided any conversations about the prospect of being wiped out financially and instead, enjoyed the good weather and a satisfactory round of golf.

"Not really," replied Vallory. I'm only driving and serving as the watch out. I assume it's not going to be too challenging. However, I did dust off my ninja outfit last night, just in case. If I had more time I'd have gotten it over to the dry cleaners."

"Girl, you are so crazy," Sandra informed her friend as she grabbed a 9-iron out of her bag and started preparing for her approach shot.

"The only thing I'm a little nervous about is Morrison showing up while we're poking around his office. Like Charles said, there is a good chance he is still in town and we know from talking to Darlene that the last time he did stop by the office he did so after normal business hours, sometime at night."

"I guess the key will be to get in and get out quickly and pray for a little luck," said Sandra. With her last practice swing out of the way, she settled over the ball and struck it perfectly, landing on the green about six feet below the pin. Vallory and Chad joined her on the green with excellent shots of their own. Bill, who had to lay up before playing to the green, brought up the rear. Ten minutes later, with three pars and Bill's bogey recorded, the group called it a round and a morning.

"What do you ladies have planned for the rest of the day?" Bill asked.

"Nothing much," said Sandra. "I need to clean my house this afternoon and we're considering going to a movie tonight to keep our minds off of the little raid going down tonight. I'm hopeful they find something that can help us turn the tables on Morrison."

"Absolutely," said Chad. "If there is anything there that can be of use, I'm confident that Charles will find it. What are you guys thinking about seeing if you do go out?"

"I don't know," replied Sandra. "I'm kind of in the mood for a good horror flick."

"What about you, Val?" asked Chad. "Any plans before Operation Money Recovery kicks off tonight?"

"Nothing much. Like Sandra, I need to clean my house a little. Besides that I'll probably try to get a little nap in later, make sure I'm bright-eyed and bushy-tailed for tonight."

Turning off S. Eastern Avenue, Charles pulled into the Best Buy parking lot. Locking his car, he walked quickly to the entrance, holding the door for a young couple before entering himself. Almost immediately he was approached by an associate.

"Can I help you find something, sir?" Considering he normally knew exactly what he wanted, he typically dismissed the attempts of salespeople, or associates as most were referred to now, and proceeded quickly to the section of the store that contained what he wanted, picked up his selected item and made his way to the nearest register. However, that wasn't the case today. He had an idea of what he wanted but he wasn't absolutely sure.

"Actually, yes. I'm looking for an external hard drive. I want to back up some files on my home computer."

"How big does the drive need to be?" she asked as she led Charles toward the section of the store that contained the computers and computer peripherals. "Any idea how much information you need to back up?"

"I'm not sure how much data he ... I have to tell you the truth."

"Hmm, 500GB would likely be enough, but just to be sure, you might want to go with a 1TB drive. That way, even if it is more than you need now, you can always back up more data later. At the end of the day, more is often better than less."

"Sounds good."

"What about power?" the associate asked.

"What do you mean?"

"You can get a hard drive that has an external power supply, which means you will need an extra outlet nearby or you can go with one that draws power via the USB port of your computer."

While he was fairly certain that finding a nearby outlet wouldn't be a problem, a hand drive that drew power via the USB port struck him as more convenient.

"Let's go with the latter," Charles quickly replied.

"You don't want to get it now?" she asked.

"The latter, not lat ... the one that draws power from the USB port."

"Here we go," she said, pointing out three different options, ranging in price from $69 to $129.

"I believe this one will work," said Charles, grabbing the middle, $89 choice. "Powered by the USB port and 1TB, yep, this should do it."

"Is there anything else I can help you with, sir?"

"No, young lady. You have been very helpful and that should do it. Thank you." Five minutes later he was back in his car, external hard drive in hand, or more accurately, the bright yellow bag.

As soon as Vallory and Charles pulled into the driveway at her home on Edgemont Drive, Darlene walked out her front door and made a beeline for the SUV.

"I guess she's ready to go," said Vallory.

"It certainly appears that way," said Charles.

Opening the door and jumping into the back seat, she greeted Vallory and Charles. "Hello Mr. Bingman and Ms. Jackson ... correct?"

"Yes, but please call me Vallory ... or just plain old Val. Ms. Jackson is my mother and far too formal for soon to be cohorts in crime."

"Good evening, Darlene, and as I said before, Charles works for me."

"Alright Vallory and Charles, I guess we are good to go."

"Just one more stop," Vallory informed her. "We need to pick up the computer guru, Paul." Heading back out to S. Eastern Boulevard, Vallory made a right and headed North. "He lives in the Frontier Rancho Estate on Rosita Drive and according to the magical GPS we will be there in about ten minutes."

Right on time, ten minutes later, they stopped in front of Mary's nephew's house; and like Darlene, he exited his home and walked toward the SUV immediately after they stopped. It appeared as if everybody was ready to go.

"Hello all," said Paul as he let himself into the SUV.

"Hello," said Charles as he proceeded to introduce himself and the ladies.

"No special tools or anything?" asked Vallory, looking back in the rearview mirror at her newest passenger.

"No, Ma'am. Everything I need is here," he said, pointing to his head, "and in these hands," as he held them up and wiggled his fingers.

"Alrighty then, I guess that does it," said Vallory as she pulled back onto Rosita Drive.

Approaching the intersection of Paradise and East Flamingo Roads, Vallory slowed down as she turned off the headlights and pulled into the Paradise Business Center. It was quiet, and thanks to some cloud cover and a couple of inoperable street lights in the area, dark. Backing her Mercedes ML 350 into the furthermost parking spot, she brought it to a stop and killed the engine. The three of them sat there is silence for the better part of a minute.

"Is everybody ready?" Charles asked.

"I guess I'm ready as I need to be," Darlene said, "I have the keys."

"Let's do this," said Paul, encouraging the group. "Unless he has a high level security system in place, which I really doubt, we should be able to access and copy whatever information he has on his computer, and it shouldn't take long at all."

"You have your phone, correct, Charles?" asked Vallory.

"I do."

"If I see anything out of the ordinary or if something happens down here that you guys need to be aware of, I'll shoot ya a text."

"Sounds good," said Charles as he grabbed the external hard drive he had purchased and opened the front passenger door. In the back, Paul and Darlene had done the same and just like that, the three would be ninjas were out of the car and walking quickly, and quietly, toward the exterior stairway that lead to the second floor and the BFSG office.

Three short minutes later, just after Darlene opened the front door, setting off the little bell positioned about the doorway, the group was standing in the BFSG lobby area. "God, that bell is annoying," Darlene whispered to the group. *It looks, and feels, so different in the stillness of the night*, Charles thought to himself. The six or seven empty desks gave the office an 'abandoned' feel, and when combined with the quiet, produced a sense of dread within its walls.

"I suppose we should start in Morrison's office," Charles whispered as he turned to the right and started moving that way. "I have to believe that is where anything of value would be found."

"Why are you whispering?" asked Paul. "Probably not necessary."

"True," Charles said, laughing at himself. "It's not like somebody is going to hear us."

"Let's get this over with," said Darlene, taking the lead and walking briskly toward Morrison's office. "I have the key for Mr. Morrison's office right here." Once inside the office, Charles moved quickly to the window, grabbed the blind wand and turned it clockwise, closing the blind tightly as possible. With the blind closed, Paul turned on the small lamp on Morrison's desk.

"Will that be enough light for you, Paul?" asked Darlene.

"That's plenty," he replied.

Down in the parking light, staring up at the office window, Vallory witnessed the faintest glow of a light come on behind the blinds. Grabbing his phone, Charles pounded out a quick text message: *to Vallory - is that light too much?* The reply was immediate: *to Charles - nope. I can barely tell that a light is on you're good.*

Within minutes Paul was seated at Morrison's desk pecking away at the keyboard. "Need anything?" asked Charles.

"Nope. Just set the hard drive down," Paul said, pointing to the corner of the desk, "I'll get to it in a minute. Thanks." As Paul continued with his effort to access Morrison's computer, Charles took a nice long look around the office; there wasn't much. In addition to desk which sat in the middle of the room, there was a paper shredder which sat next to it, a four drawer filing cabinet in one corner and an L-shaped sofa in the other. "Well, not much here, shouldn't take long to search everything," Charles mumbled mainly to himself in the dimly lit room.

"Excuse me, what was that?" asked Darlene.

"Nothing really. I was noting that it shouldn't take too long. Just talking to myself I guess."

"How long is this going to take?" Darlene asked. "I certainly hope we can be out of here in the next 10 minutes or so."

"That shouldn't be a problem for me, Darlene. There doesn't appear to be a lot to search through."

"I'm in," Paul mentioned nonchalantly from behind Morrison's desk as he unpacked the hard drive. "What do you want?" Charles.

"Pardon me?"

"Is there anything specifically you are looking for from this computer? Any specific data. Any specific files?"

"I'm not sure exactly what we're looking for. How much data is there?"

"Hmm, looks like 45.7 GB spread across 95,096 files. It appears as if you got a lot more external storage than you needed."

"Well I'd rather have too much than not enough. How long will it take to copy it all?"

"Impossible to know exactly, but based on the processor, the rotational speed of the drives and the computer's cache, I would guess between 15 - 20 minutes."

"Twenty minutes!?" Darlene exclaimed.

"At the most I suspect," replied Paul.

"Make sure we take that trash, the packaging from the hard drive, with us," said Charles. "We don't want to leave anything behind."

"Not a problem."

Grabbing the handle and pulling the top drawer of the filing cabinet, Charles was relieved to find that it was open. However, his relief quickly turned to disappointment. Going through the first three drawers, the fourth was empty, all he found was information on clients and their accounts: names, phone numbers, home addresses, email addresses, beneficiaries and things along those lines. Items one would expect to find in a filing cabinet. He took little comfort in the fact that all of the paperwork was neatly filed and apparently well maintained. There was no smoking gun. Nothing to shed light on where Morrison was or what he may have done with their money.

Sensing his disappointment, Paul informed Charles that the desk drawers, three on either side, were open. Making his way over to the desk, he ripped open the top drawer on the right side only to find standard office supplies: staples, paperclips, pens, pencils and thumb tacks. Nothing of any substance was found in the other two drawers. Making his way behind Paul, to the other side of the desk, he started with the bottom drawer on the left side.

"Looks like we're about halfway there," Paul informed his co-conspirators.

"Thank, God," said Darlene. "I am ready to get the hell out of here ... excuse my French."

"It won't be long now," Charles assured her, taking a break and looking up from his search. Opening the middle drawer, Charles was disappointed to see that it was empty, except for the two or three dust balls. Pulling the top, and last drawer, Charles immediately spotted a group of letters; six or seven in all. Each had already been opened. Running his finger along the top seam of the first one, he reached in and pulled out the contents; a letter from Bank of the West. Reading through the letter quickly, it was apparent that Morrison had failed to make a scheduled payment on a loan. *Must be the loan Darlene had referenced*, he thought. The second envelope contained an earlier letter from Bank of the West which addressed the same loan.

"Just about finished," Paul said, looking toward Darlene who had planted herself near the door.

"I'll just take all of these and look them over in detail later," Charles said, as much to himself as anyone.

Seeing that Darlene was clearly growing more anxious, Charles made his way from the desk to the door where she stood. "How long have you been with Morrison?"

"Excuse me?"

"How long have you worked with Morrison here at BFSG?"

"Nearly from the beginning, sixteen years. I started with him about a year after he started the company. During that first year, his wife, Adele, handled most of the administrative stuff. He couldn't really afford to hire anyone else. However, as the business grew, he started to bring more people on board."

"Did you know him before you started work here?"

"No. I had worked briefly with his wife at a small company called Shuliman Industries, an import and export company."

"A merchant?" Charles asked.

"No, an EMC."

"EMC?"

"An export management company. EMCs handle export operations for a domestic company that wants to sell its product overseas but doesn't know how. The EMC does it all, the hiring of dealers, distributors and representatives; handling advertising, marketing and promotions; overseeing marking and packaging; arranging shipping; and sometimes arranging financing. In some cases, the EMC even takes title to the goods, in essence becoming its own distributor. EMCs usually specialize by product, foreign market or both.

"Interesting."

"It can be. I started as a receptionist and worked my way into the Human Resources department, where I became an assistant manager. Adele worked there as an accountant. We knew each other but not that well. I ran into her about two years after she left the company at a garage sale. She told me about her husband's company and the fact that they were looking to hire an administrative assistant. I didn't know much about finance, but considering my work as a receptionist and background in HR, she thought I would be a great fit ... and she had grown tired of working with her husband. I met with him two days later, started the following Monday and I have been here since. As they say, the rest is history."

"That's it," said Paul as he disconnected the external hard drive and began to return Morrison's computer to the way he had found it. "I have no idea if you will find anything that will help you, but you have all the files that were on his computer," as he handed the hard drive to Charles, who had walked back over to the desk.

"Sounds good, Paul." With the letters in his pocket and the hard drive in hand he was ready to go and started making his way to the door. "What about the trash can?" asked Paul. Looking back, Charles spotted the small trash can on the left side of the desk. *How could I have missed it?* he thought. Just as he turned and headed back toward the trash can, his phone informed him of a text message: *from Vallory - how much longer?* Stopping short of the trash can he responded quickly: *to Vallory - two or three minutes.*

The top layer of trash was mostly candy wrappers and a couple discarded magazines. Just under the second magazine Charles spotted a piece of crumbled up paper. Fishing it out and straightening it out on the desk, he saw that it was an itinerary. His eyes immediately noted the name, destination and date: Carlton F. Morrison III, Aruba and October 8th, six days from now. "Damn it," Charles cursed under his breath. "I'll be damned!" Reaching for the desk lamp, he found the switch it and turned it off. Waiting a minute for his eyes to adjust to the new level of darkness, he carefully made his way to the window and returned the blind to the way he had found it.

"I've got the packaging from the hard drive," Paul informed him. "No trash shall be left behind." With his eyes fully adjusted, Charles turned and walked purposefully toward the office door where Paul and Darlene, with keys in hand, waited. Pulling the door closed, Darlene quickly locked it.

"What's down the hall?" Charles asked Darlene.

"Not much, just a bathroom and a small kitchenette. Nothing really to see."

"Sounds good." Stepping outside the exterior doorway, Darlene turned and locked the door once Charles and Paul had passed. With the door locked behind them, the three cohorts made a beeline for the stairs. Moments later with the ninjas back in the car, Vallory turned her SUV onto Paradise Road and hit the gas, more forcefully than she intended, resulting in a squealing of the tires.

"Yikes, a little Bo and Luke Duke action," she joked.

"Who?" Paul asked.

"*The Dukes of Hazzard.* You know, Bo and Luke, Daisy, Uncle Jesse, Gener ... " The blank stare told Charles all he needed to know. "Never mind."

Friday night. For the second time in three nights the group gathered at Dave and Mary's. As to be expected, they were anxious to find about what had been found at Morrison's office. Tonight they were joined by Darlene and her husband, Robert. The introductions were short as Darlene had met everyone at one time or another at the BFSG office, and of course, everyone except Dave and Mary knew her. "I invited Darlene and Robert to join us, first because they asked, but more importantly, because like six of the people in our group, they have a financial stake in whatever actions we take next. Anyone have any issues with that?"

"Nope. I think it's a good idea," said Sandra. "Darlene and Robert ...

"Bob is fine," Robert quickly noted.

"Darlene and Bob certainly do have a stake and I'm sure any insight Darlene can offer with respect to Morrison or BFSG will be helpful." The other friends quickly agreed.

"So, let's get down to it. How did it go?" asked Chad, kicking off the conversation.

"Well, a couple of things. First, we were able to access Morrison's computer and copy all of his files," said Charles, holding up the external hard drive. Paul was tremendous, Mary. Make sure you thank him again for all of us."

"I will."

"While I did briefly look through the files earlier today, I haven't had a chance to dive into them too deeply. In fact, I thought it would speed things up if we split up the workload. I went ahead and picked up some thumb drives earlier today and split the files between them." Reaching into his pocket, Charles pulled out the four thumb drives. "Each drive contains around 20,000 files, give or take. One for Bill and Chad, one for Dave, one for George and Sandra and one for Vallory," he noted as he handed one to each of his friends.

"Is there anything specifically we should be looking for?" asked George.

"I'm glad you asked," said Charles. That is a perfect segue to the second finding last night. While nothing out of the ordinary was found in his filing cabinet, I did find some letters in his desk drawer and a flight itinerary crumbled up in a trash can. I was able to discern from a few of the letters that BFSG's corporate banking account is with Bank of the West and Morrison is currently delinquent on a $3 million loan."

"Holy shit," said Bill. "A $3 million loan!?"

"I had no idea he could even get a loan that large," Darlene whispered to Vallory.

"Yep," Charles confirmed, "and it appears as if the bank is prepared to take action within the next week if the loan is not serviced, which leads to the flight itinerary."

"Where and when?" asked Chad.

"Aruba on Wednesday morning," answered Charles. "Put those pieces of information together and it appears as if Morrison is planning to disappear just before the bank comes a calling on that loan." For a long time the group just sat there, silent, most with their heads hung low.

"It seems to me that is our opening," said Vallory.

"What do you mean?" asked Chad. "It seems to me it is more a case of the door closing."

"The itinerary seems to confirm what we suspected, which is that Morrison is still in the area, he hasn't run yet. That's good. If he was simply bent on stealing the money, if this was a simple case of greed, he likely would have disappeared with it all by now. You know the truth is, I've been thinking a lot about this situation and quite frankly, it appears to me that if there has been any greed, we have been the guilty parties."

"Excuse me," said Bill. "You think we're guilty of being greedy?"

"Yes."

"I think Vallory is right, Bill. Six percent returns guaranteed ... monthly?" It always struck me as likely too good to be true. However, the statements always indicated the returns were there, and on the few occasions George and I did request funds from Morrison, there weren't any problems," said Sandra.

"I have to agree with Vallory and Sandra," said Charles. After speaking with my daughter during my last visit and giving it some thought, greed was not a sin exclusive to Morrison. I believe it was E. A. Bucchianeri who said, *'It was not curiosity that killed the goose who laid the golden egg, but an insatiable greed that devoured common sense.'* If we're honest with ourselves, I think we have to acknowledge that in our pursuit of financial gains, we have not used common sense and good judgment." Though no one spoke, as Charles looked around the room he saw lots of heads moving up and down, excluding Bill's. It appeared as if he wasn't entirely convinced.

"As I was saying," Vallory continued, "if he was simply bent on stealing the money, if this was a simple case of greed, he likely would have disappeared with it all by now. After all, there was really nothing stopping him. Heck, there still isn't. Maybe he is still looking for a way to maintain his business, continue running BFSG and pay back the loan before the bank takes action. What do you guys think?"

"I think you may be right, Vallory," offered Charles. If his only intent was to abscond with stolen money, it seems to me he would have done so by now. The fact that he hasn't suggests his preference would be to somehow work his way through this issue with the loan and continue running BFSG. If we're right, we use that motivation against him to get our money back before he does disappear."

"Sounds reasonable," said George. "The question becomes, how do we manipulate him into giving us access to our money, and more importantly, get it done within the next four days?"

"That's what we need to determine tonight," said Charles. "That's what we need to figure out right now. Any ideas?"

After a long silence, Mary was the first to speak. "It seems to me that we have to use his fear, his desperation against him. If we assume he is looking for a big deal, something that will bring in significant money ... quickly, we have to dangle some bait and hope he bites. When we look at the numbers, what do we know for certain, Charles?"

"As I said, Morrison has an outstanding $3 million loan. Based on my reading of one of the letters, the loan period is 60 months at a 3% rate. That works out to monthly payments of $57,963.70. Another letter stated that the loan was three months past due, which gives you $173,891.11. However, there is a fixed $10,500 fee for any late payment. You tack on another $31,500 and you are looking at $205,391.11 that is owed right now."

"That is a lot of damn money," said Vallory.

"Previously," Charles continued, "we figured Morrison was managing about $3.75 million between the six of us ... "

"And $55,600 of our money," added Darlene as her husband nodded his head in agreement.

"Unfortunately," Charles continued, "what we don't know is how much of that is in jeopardy. It seems to me that at a minimum we need to dangle enough to make him believe he can get right on the loan. He needs to believe the made up deal we're going to put before him will solve his problem. On the other end of the spectrum, I suppose there is no maximum amount we could dangle in front of him. However, I believe there is a danger in trying to go too big. Something along the lines of a $10 million deal might be too aggressive and scare him off."

"Seems pretty straight forward to me," said Bill. "We need to come up with a good, plausible long con."

"A long con?" asked Mary.

"You know, like in the *Ocean's Eleven* movie."

"And *Ocean's Twelve* and *Ocean's Thirteen*," added Vallory.

"I prefer the original, made in the early 60s, with Frank Sinatra and Dean Martin," said Bill.

"Wasn't Sammy Davis, Jr. also in the original?" asked Sandra.

"He was," Vallory replied, "along with Cesar Romero, Peter Lawford and Angie Dickinson."

"Anyway," Charles said, "the long con, Mary, refers to a con which requires more planning, preparation and a longer period of time to execute. Additionally, the long con requires a large crew, like ours, to pull off the deception ... and that, my friends, is exactly what we need to do. Let's put our heads together and figure this out. Agreed?" Charles asked. He was greeted with nine vigorous, affirmative nods. Two and a half hours later, after their long con, dubbed Operation Money Recovery, had been developed and reviewed - three times from beginning to end - and everyone understood their respective roles, they called it a night.

[7] LAYING THE FOUNDATION

Saturday morning. "Well it's a good thing it's early," said Chad as Bill pulled off of E. Lake Mead Parkway into the Walmart parking lot.

"Absolutely," agreed Bill. "Nothing worse than trying to navigate through jam-packed aisles, bouncing off other customers, as you're trying to shop." They pulled into a spot near the front of the sparsely populated parking lot and hurried to the entrance. "Back that way," said Bill, pointing toward the 'Electronics' sign hanging in the back of the store, to the left. They rarely shopped at Walmart and they never shopped this early. However, they had their marching orders from the meeting last night and they needed to pick up a disposable pre-paid phone as soon as possible and they figured Walmart was as good as any place to get one. Arriving in the Electronics Section, an associate greeted them.

"How can I help you, gentlemen?"

"We're looking for a disposable pre-paid phone."

"Right this way. Is there a specific phone or model you're looking for?" the associate asked as they reached a glass case filled with phones.

"Not really ... um, Rafael" said Bill, squinting slightly to read the young man's name tag.

"Something pretty basic. We don't need a lot of frills."

"I've never owned one, but I have heard good things about this model and it gets good reviews," Rafael said as he pointed to an AT&T GoPhone. Pulling it out of the case, he handed it to Bill. "You can surf the Internet, take pictures, text and send email. Pretty much the basic functions you would want in a phone."

"That's sounds good to me," said Chad.

"If you're lookin' for a good pre-paid, that is a pretty good phone to go with."

"What's the price, Rafael?"

"That phone is $39.99."

"Well the price is definitely right," said Bill. "We'll take it. Now how do we go about activating service?"

"That's pretty straight forward. You can do that on AT& T's website. The address and instructions are in the box. You will also need to buy a instant pre-paid minutes & data card," he said, pointing to an adjacent case filled with cards.

"I don't imagine we will need to use this for more than a few days which will probably amount to less than a few hours."

"In that case I would just go with a $15 card," suggested Rafael.

"Sounds good," said Bill. "That's what we'll do, go with a $15 card."

"Anything else, gentlemen?"

"That should do it," said Bill.

"Great, I can ring you up right over here," said Rafael as he led them to a nearby register.

"What are you doing, Sandra?" George called out to his wife from the kitchen as he prepared a late breakfast.

"I just got a text from Bill with the phone number I needed, so I'm finishing up the letter we discussed last night," Sandra called out.

"No need to yell," said George softly, appearing in the doorway.

"Oh shit!" she said, turning to look at her husband. "You scared me. I thought you were still in the kitchen."

"Done already, huh?"

"Yep. Finished just now. What do you think?" she asked as she grabbed the letter off the printer and handed it to her husband. After taking a moment to read through it a couple of times, George reported that the letter looked good.

"It looks pretty damn good to me. It addresses all the points we discussed. Nice job, Babe."

"Thank you. Now I just need to put it in this envelope so that Charles can place it in Morrison's desk drawer."

"Sounds good to me. They're going back tonight, correct?"

"Yep. We only have a few days to try and pull this off; no time to waste."

"So let me get this right. This real estate group ... "

"Helix."

"Yeah, Helix Real Estate Group is a real company that we're co-opting."

"Yep. The group and the Business Development President, Jordan Malone, are both very real. The only thing that was changed with respect to contact information was the phone number; that belongs to Bill, the one he just gave me. In fact, Charles found correspondence between Morrison and Malone when he went through Morrison's computer files."

"So the Helix Real Estate Group is not unknown to him?" Pulling over the small chair that normally sat against the wall, George took a seat and listened intently as his wife continued.

"Nope. Only two potential problems as I see it. First, we have to hope that when Morrison finds the letter he calls, vice jumping in his car and driving over to their offices. If he does, it's game over. Obviously no one there would have any idea what the hell he is talking about."

"I think it's reasonable to expect that he'll call first," said George. "He's a business man and this is twenty-first century. The telephone, email and text messages are the ways everyone communicates today, even us older folks."

"Second, we have to hope he has never spoken to Malone. If he bites, we have to assume that at some point he'll call. The good thing is, Darlene does not recall Malone, or anyone from the Helix Real Estate Group in fact, calling or stopping by the BFSG office. We have every reason to believe that their correspondence has been limited to mail, electronic and the snail type."

In spite of the late meeting last night and considering the precarious financial position he, along with his friends, appeared to be in, Charles had slept like a baby last night. The new mattress he recently purchased was already paying dividends. *Probably my best night of sleep in a month*, he thought. It looked like a beautiful morning, with slight cloud cover that would hold the temperature down a bit, so he figured he would take advantage of it and get in a nice run, at least four miles. After getting a drink of water he made his way back to his bedroom and slipped on his newest running shoes. Two minutes later he was out the door and stretching on the front side walk. Just as he was about to take off, he realized he had forgot something and ran back into the house. After grabbing his iPod and headphones off his dresser he turned around and headed back toward the front door. Closing it forcefully behind him, he took off at a leisurely pace and quickly settled into a nice rhythm.

Making the turn at the two-mile point, he checked his watch and noted that he was on a 8½ minute-mile pace. *Not too bad*, he thought, taking a deep breath as he prepared to step it up a little and increase his speed. He felt strong. There was very little traffic on the street this morning and quiet. It was perfect. As he knocked out the third mile right on pace, he found himself singing *Gimme Shelter* along with Mick. *Great, great song*, he thought. *Hell. the entire 'Let it Bleed' album was great!*

Fifteen minutes later, after finishing the last mile 12 seconds ahead of pace and a nice walk to cool down, he was walking back through his front door. He considered sitting for a few minutes in the living room but changed his mind and instead, made a beeline for the kitchen. Reaching into the cupboard next to the refrigerator, he pulled out his blender and a large cup. The last two bananas on the counter were looking pretty rough and he had some fruit and broccoli that he wanted to use up; a smoothie should hit the spot this morning. Grabbing the remote control off the breakfast bar, he turned the television on and changed the channel to Bloomberg TV.

William Riley, the host, was speaking to his guest about the Federal Reserve:

> Riley: "Just as Fed Chair Janet Yellen and her cohorts rapidly approach making a decision regarding raising interest rates, it appears as if their two mandates will probably pull them in two completely different directions."
>
> Guest: "Exactly, Bill. By June, the jobless rate will likely have fallen to about 5.1 percent, a rate the policy makers consider to be full employment. Contrast that with the Federal Reserve's preferred inflation gauge which will likely not have budged from its current 1.4 percent. As the jobless rate falls it is bound to push up wages - higher than most believe I suspect - which will trigger a move by many companies to start charging more for their products and services."
>
> Riley: "So, to which consideration, jobs or inflation, will the Fed give greater weight?"
>
> Guest: "I believe that ultimately employment is the primary consideration in the Fed's policy-making process. There is no doubt they would love to see that unemployment number come down. My sense is that they would like to drive that rate down to 5%."

As Riley and his guest dug down deeper into the weeds on unemployment and inflation, Charles gathered all the ingredients for his smoothie, combining an orange, some Greek yogurt, a peach, a little ice and some protein powder to go with the bananas and broccoli. After giving the mixture a 30-second blend he poured the drink into his glass, grabbed a straw, walked over to the living room, and after kicking off his shoes, plopped down on the sofa, sinking into the overstuffed cushions.

After an hour and a half of television, Charles figured it was late enough in the morning to make the requisite phone calls to Sandra and Paul. He needed to call Sandra to see if she had finished composing the letter and if so, find out when would be a good time to pick it up; and he needed to speak with Paul to find out what time he would be available tonight, to return to the BFSG office. Charles imagined the young man's computer skills and knowledge would prove to be invaluable. *Hell*, he thought, *they have already proved to be invaluable.*

Picking up her phone immediately after the first ring, Sandra informed Charles that she was finished with the letter and he could pick it up at any time before six as she and George had dinner reservations at 6:30. Minutes after hanging up with Sandra, Charles dialed Paul; disappointingly, the phone immediately went to voicemail:

> "Hello Paul, it's Charles Bingman. I believe your aunt spoke to you about the need to make a return visit to the BFSG office tonight. When you have a moment, please give me a call to let me know what time you will be available and I can let you know what we have in mind. Thanks and we'll talk soon."

With his phone calls out of the way, Charles grabbed the remote control and turned the channel to the 70's music station. As he set the remote down and turned to head for his bedroom, and a shower, he recognized the first few notes of *Signed, Sealed, Delivered I'm Yours* from Stevie Wonder. Making a quick U-turn, he grabbed the remote and turned the volume. *Great song.*

"What are you thinking about?" Mary asked her husband as they sat on their back patio enjoying a little lunch and the warmth of the early afternoon sun as the early cloud cover had dissipated.

"Just thinking about the plan that was put into place last night. Just wondering if there is anything that may have been overlooked."

"Come up with anything?"

"Nope. It seems to me the plan is pretty solid. Its success is somewhat dependent upon Morrison acting out of greedy motives, but I guess that is often the case with this type of gambit. If he was completely rationale and trustworthy, we wouldn't be where we are."

"So true. You're right. Have you taken care of your part of the plan yet?"

"I have. Right before lunch I established an alias with a new email address." Reaching out his hand to his wife, Dave said, "hello, I'm David J. Welles and I can be reached at david.j.welles@desertmail.com."

"Where did you get 'Welles' from?"

"Orson Welles."

"Well that's interesting, and what does the 'J' stand for? I'm surprised you didn't go with 'R' for Rosebud."

"I have no idea, I just pulled the 'J' out of my ass. What's a good 'J' name?"

"How about Jeffrey?"

"Nah."

"How about Jerome?"

"God no! I hate that name."

"It's a pretend name, Dear. Does it really matter?"

"No, but how about something else. Even if it's a pretend name I want to like it."

"You are impossible. How about, Jules?"

"Like Jules from *Pulp Fiction*?"

"*Pulp Fiction*?"

"Yeah, you know, Samuel L. Jackson's character."

"I was thinking of Jules Verne, the author. I wasn't thinking of *Pulp Fiction* or the Samuel L. Jackson character - even thought I like him - but sure, if it works for you."

"It does. Let's go with David Jules Welles."

"If it works for you, um, David, it works for me."

Reaching for his phone, Charles tried Paul for a second time. The young computer guru picked up immediately. "This is Paul."

"Hello, Paul. This is Charles"

"How goes it, Chuck?"

"Not too bad, and you?"

"No complaints, my friend. I did speak to my aunt and she let me know the plan; I think I know what you guys have in mind."

"Good. Is that a problem?"

"Nope. It should be easy enough. Tonight is a tough night though as I have other plans I can't get out of. If you guys don't mind going later, say 10:30 - 11:00 p.m., we can do it then. I don't have any plans for tomorrow night if you want to wait until then."

"No, we don't want to wait until tomorrow. We can do it at any time tonight that works for you; we really need to get this first piece of the plan into place tonight, no matter how late. Say we pick you up about 10:45?"

"Sure. That will work."

"Great, I will shoot you a text when we are 10 - 15 minutes out."

"Sounds good, Chuck. We'll see you guys tonight."

Chuck, huh? It had been a long time since anyone called him Chuck, he thought. He was somewhat ambivalent about the use of the shortened name. While 'Charles' often sounded too formal, 'Chuck' just as often came across as just the opposite, too informal. *Oh well, there is no harm in letting Paul go with Chuck*. Hanging up, Charles immediately opened his phone's messaging app. He figured now was as good a time as any to go pick up the letter from Sandra: *to Sandra - I can be by in 10 minutes to pick up the letter if ...* . Before he had a chance to finish, the doorbell rang. Making his way to the door, he was surprised to see George and Sandra standing there. "Hey, what a surprise, I was just sending you a text about that letter. Come on in."

"Thanks, Charles but we just wanted to drop this off," Sandra said as she reached into her purse and handed him the letter in question. "We've got some running around to do this afternoon and thought we'd drop this off before we headed out. We just wanted to make sure you got this before tonight."

"Perfect. Like I said, I was just sending you a text, about the letter, and I just spoke to Mary's nephew, Paul, and we're good to go for tonight."

"Sounds great," George said, "it looks like the first part of the plan is right on track. Well, we have to go, but you guys be careful tonight."

"Will do. I'll talk to you guys soon. Take care."

"What about a voicemail greeting?" Chad asked.

"What do you mean?" asked Bill as a quizzical look spread across his face.

"Well, you're supposed to be Malone. What happens if Morrison calls tomorrow night or after normal business hours? He needs to hear a professional sounding message."

"Ahh, I see what you mean. That should be easy enough. I'll just make up something real quick."

"Better yet, let's call the Helix Real Estate Group office. It's Saturday night and no one should be there; that will give us a chance to hear their greeting if we call now."

"Sounds good. What if it's a woman's voice on the message?"

"Well, I guess if we are going to make this as real as possible, we would need to have one of the women - Val, Sandra or Mary - create the message. Got something to write with? Let's write down the message verbatim. We don't want to miss anything."

"Hold on. Let me go grab some paper and a pen."

"While you're grabbing those, let me get online and find the number for their offices." Three minutes later, with pen and paper; and the speakerphone engaged, Bill dialed the Helix Real Estate Group office. After four rings, it went to voicemail:

> "Thank you for calling the Helix Real Estate Group, the premiere real estate services company in Southern Nevada for more than 30 years. Our normal business hours are Monday through Friday, 8:30 a.m. to 5:00 p.m. Thank you for taking the time to contact us. We look forward to speaking with you. Please leave a brief message, including your name and number, and we will contact you soon."

"Well, it was a male voice, so that's good. Did you get the entire message?" Chad asked.

"Yep. Too easy. So which one of us should set up our voicemail message?"

"Probably you. You've got a little more bass in your voice and your diction is good."

"Alright, I'll do it." Ten minutes and four attempts later - in an effort to get it just right - they finished their mimicked message.

In a scene that was highly reminiscent of two nights ago, Vallory and Charles pulled into the driveway of Bob and Darlene's home on Edgemont Drive. The only differences being that it was significantly later, and tonight, Bob escorted his wife out to Vallory's SUV. After salutations all the way around, Bob and Darlene shared a kiss and then the three of them departed to pick up Paul, the fourth member of their crew for this night's mission. Grabbing his phone, Charles composed a brief text message: *to Paul - on the way.*

Heading back out to S. Eastern Boulevard, Vallory made the familiar right and headed North. Ten minutes later they were parked in Paul's driveway. Glancing at his watch, "10:45, right on time," Charles noted. After a couple of minutes and no Paul, Vallory suggested they go tap on his front door. "I'll give him another minute or two and then I'll go to the door." As they waited, Charles decided to send a text: *to Paul - we're outside.* After two minutes, and no Paul, Charles jumped out, walked quickly to the door, and rang the doorbell. A minute, and a firm knock later, still no Paul. Charles was getting a little nervous. *This phase of the plan absolutely requires Paul and his unique skill set*, he thought. *Where the fuck is he?*

Just as Charles reached for the doorbell a second time, the front door swung open and there stood Paul, decked out from head to toe in black. "Sorry about that, Chuck. I just got home a few minutes ago and I had to drop a load and get changed."

"You realize that is probably a little TMI, don't you?" Charles asked the young man. Ignoring the question, Paul headed to the SUV where Vallory and Darlene waited, with Charles right behind him.

"Sorry about the short delay ladies," said Paul as he climbed in. "Good to see both of you again."

"Not a problem," Vallory assured him. "We're just glad you could make it tonight. Well, it looks like we have everyone, let's go get this done."

"Let's do it again," said Darlene.

"That's funny," Vallory chuckled, almost inaudibly.

"What's that, Val?" Charles asked.

"I was just thinking of that old Sidney Poitier and Bill Cosby movie, *Let's Do It Again* ... mid-70's."

"Never heard of it," said Darlene.

"I remember it," said Charles. Funny movie.

"Mid-70's?" said Paul. "Way before my time."

"Poitier and Cosby play a couple of blue-collar workers, in Atlanta if memory serves me right, who are looking for a way to raise funds for their fraternal order. In order to do so, they travel to New Orleans and rig a boxing match by hypnotizing a skinny boxer, Jimmy 'J.J.' Walker from *Good Times*, turning him into a super-fighter. They bet big and win big. However, once the gangsters - who lost big - realize they were conned, all hell breaks loose. Poitier and Cosby have to rig another fight, hence the title *Let's Do It Again*, but this time the con is run so the gangster's can get their money back. Funny, funny stuff," said Vallory.

"Well it won't be too funny if we don't get our money back," Charles said.

"Bob and I don't have the kind of money at stake as the rest of you, but it will kill us financially if we can't recover our money. This definitely isn't funny."

"Agreed," said Vallory. "There is nothing funny about losing money you have worked hard for over 30 years or more and will depend on in retirement."

Just like two nights ago, Vallory slowed down as she turned off the headlights and pulled into the Paradise Business Center. Backing her Mercedes ML 350 into the same spot, she brought it to a stop and killed the engine. Just as they started to get out, one of Las Vegas' finest drove by in a patrol car. The patrol car's brake lights flashed briefly and the group held their collective breath. Completing a U-turn, the lights on the police cruiser came on, flooding the area with blue and red lights. Quickly accelerating, the cruiser sped away, proceeding back up Paradise Road. Slowly exhaling, "We're good," said Charles.

Exiting the SUV, Charles, Darlene and Paul made their way to the now familiar exterior stairway and proceeded up the stairs, to the BFSG Suite. "Let's get in there and get this over with," said Darlene as she first opened the exterior door, and then moving quickly, opened the door to Morrison's office. As soon as the door was open, Paul headed to Morrison's desk and turned on the desktop lamp before settling in the high back office chair. He immediately got to work after briefly extending his arms, interlocking his hands and cracking his knuckles.

To his left, Charles placed the letter from the Helix Real Estate Group in the bottom of the drawer, under a couple pieces of loose paper; and finished by replacing the stack of letters he had taken the other night, on top.

"I guess we won't need those anymore," noted Darlene who had remained by the office door.

"No, I don't believe we will," noted Charles. "I think we gathered all the useful information that we could have from them and we need Morrison to find the Helix letter with his other pieces of mail. Besides, just in case, I made copies of each of the letters earlier today."

"Smart. Sounds wise," said Darlene.

"Yep, every once in awhile I have a good idea."

"Well, that's it," said Paul.

"You're already finished?" asked Darlene, grateful he had finished so quickly, but not quite believing Paul.

"Yep. Not really a whole lot to it. I'm ready to go." Just like that, the chair was pushed back into place, the lamp turned off and the office doors locked. Eight minutes after they had left Vallory alone in the parking lot, they had returned.

"Well that was fast," Vallory said as all three climbed back into the SUV.

"Not a lot to it," said Charles.

"Nope," agreed Paul.

"Alrighty then, that was fun," Vallory said as she turned her SUV onto Paradise Road, making a hasty exit.

[8] THE APPROACH

Sunday morning. Finishing up her breakfast, Darlene placed her dirty dishes in the sink and moseyed over to the coffee maker at the end of the counter, pouring the last little bit of coffee into her mug. While she would have preferred a full mug, this was the last of it and she had no desire to brew another pot. Bob had left twenty minutes ago, headed to Summit Fitness over on E. Russell Road to meet Bryan, his best friend since high school, for their regularly scheduled racquetball match. While she normally cherished the personal quiet time his absence offered every Sunday morning, she was feeling anxious today and she really wished he has home. However, he wasn't here and the time had come to carry out her small part of the operation. Finishing up her coffee, she dropped the mug in the sink and reached into the pocket of her robe, pulling out her cell phone.

Taking a deep breath, she dialed the number; prepared to deliver her lines from the script she had developed with Charles. She was ready to deliver them directly to Mr. Morrison or to voicemail. After the third ring, she was fairly certain, as she had predicted, that Mr. Morrison was not going to answer his cell phone. Drawing a deep breath and exhaling slowly, she listened as the phone rang for the fourth time. Following the fifth ring, Mr. Morrison's voice came on the line, encouraging her to leave a message. Following the familiar beep, she did exactly that:

> "Hello Mr. Morrison, this is Darlene. I hope you are well and enjoying the time with your son and grandchildren. I'm sorry to bother you on a Sunday; however, a Mr. Malone, with the Helix Real Estate Group, has left a couple messages at the office asking you to contact him. He wanted to know if you had a chance to consider their offer, outlined in a letter sent last month. I wanted to be sure you got this message as he seemed awfully adamant that he talk to you soon. He suggested that there was a limited time to act. Well, take care and I will see you soon."

Twenty minutes later, glancing at his phone, Morrison saw that he had missed a call and there was a voicemail message. Tapping the 'Play' icon, he listened intently. "Letter. What letter?" Morrison asked the empty room. He had corresponded with a Malone - John? Jason? something like that - in the past, but he didn't recall seeing any letter outlining a proposal recently. He waited an hour, then he returned Darlene's call. He had wanted to reach out to her before Monday anyway.

Unbeknown to Charles and Vallory, they were parked in the exact same sport Morrison was a few days earlier as he watched his administrative assistant leave the office for the day. They had immediately made their way here once Darlene apprised them that she had left the scripted message on Morrison's cell phone. They had no idea when, or if, he would show up. Not only did they not know when he would check his phone messages, hell, they weren't even sure he was anywhere near Las Vegas; they assumed so but they definitely weren't sure.

Sitting out here could end up being a complete waste of time. If Morrison didn't stop by his office they had no way of confirming if he was still in town and if he would bite on the bait they were dangling. Oh well, nothing to do for now but to sit back and relax. "What are you thinking about, Charles?"

"Not a whole lot really. Just hoping that Morrison shows up and trying to prepare myself mentally for a long day. Let's see, it's almost 10:30 a.m. now and we're not scheduled to get relieved by Dave and Mary until 6:00 tonight. Let's hope he shows up before then."

Dialing Darlene's cell phone, Morrison waited for her to pick up ... she never did. *Just as well*, he thought, and left a message:

> "Hello, Darlene. I got your message. Thank you. Great to hear from you as I was planning to call you later today anyway. I have decided to stay with my son and his family for just a few more days. The time off has given me a chance to relax and recharge my batteries. I may be in the office by the end of the week, but if not, certainly by the following Monday. I will reach out to Mr. Malone when I return. Thanks again."

Immediately after listening to the voicemail, Darlene called Charles. "Hello, Darlene. What do you got?"

" I just heard from Morrison. Like you instructed, I didn't answer when he called, I just let it go straight to voicemail so we could be sure of exactly what was said. He said that he got my message about Malone, he would reach out to Malone when he returned and that he was planning to stay with his son a little longer; possibly as long as a week from tomorrow."

"Hmm, interesting," said Charles. Well, we know that he's not staying with his son, that's a lie; however, that doesn't necessarily mean he's still here in the area. Did he show any interest in the news about Malone?"

"To tell you the truth, if he was intrigued in any way, I couldn't really tell. He just matter-of-factly stated that he would 'reach out' when he came back to work."

"Well that's a little disconcerting. I guess we'll just wait and see. If he is in town and the prospect of a deal has piqued his interest, he'll show up. If not, on either count, he won't. It's that simple. Nothing we can do at this point but to wait. Thanks, Darlene. We'll let you and the rest of the crew know if we see anything."

To say the first four hours were uneventful would be an understatement on a grand scale. Absolutely nothing happened. There was very moderate traffic on the streets and essentially no traffic in or out of the Paradise Business Center. That wasn't much of a surprise considering it was Sunday; a very lazy Sunday afternoon in fact.

"Well fortunately your SUV is comfortable, Val. I guess it could be worse."

"Based on what I paid for this thing, the least it could do is be comfortable. I'm waiting for them to come out with a model that gives you a pedicure when you're parked."

"With self-driving vehicles right around the corner, the auto-pedicure can't be too far behind," Charles deadpanned. The friends got a good chuckle out of their silliness, and in fact, managed to enjoy good conversation and progressively sillier jokes for most of the long afternoon.

At 2:46 p.m., just as Vallory was starting to drift off a little, Charles nudged her shoulder and asked rhetorically, "what do we have here? Darlene said Morrison drove a dark blue Infiniti didn't she?"

"Yeah, a dark blue Infiniti, that's right." The car Charles was looking at had pulled into the Paradise Business Center parking lot, the first car in at least an hour and a half, and drove slowly toward the end where the BFSG office was located.

"That looks like a Nissan Maxima," Vallory said, "not an Infiniti; plus it looks black, not dark blue to me."

"I don't know," Charles said, "I think this may be him. The vehicle suddenly stopped and two younger males jumped out and walked slowly around the car as if inspecting it.

"Flat tire," Vallory guessed. "It looks like they believe they may have a flat tire. A minute later, after conducting a 360 degree inspection of their vehicle, and apparently satisfied that there wasn't a problem with a tire or anything else, they jumped back in the car and took off.

"Man I was hoping that was him."

"I know, my friend. I know. Have faith. He'll show up sooner or later."

"Well it's too late for sooner, now it's only a question of how much later," said Charles, sounding quite dejected to Vallory.

With her foot on the brake, Vallory quickly tapped her car's start button, turning the sound system on. On the steering wheel, she selected the CD player. Moments later, a slightly throaty male voice continued a narration. "Do you mind?" asked Vallory.

"No, what is it?"

"It's the Audio CD of *The Millionaire Next Door*. I just started listening to it a few days ago. I read it a long time ago, probably 12 or 13 years, but I have wanted to read it again. Instead of 'reading' it though, I figured I would try listening to it this time. I had never tried one of these audio CDs. Great book. Ever read it?"

"No. heard of it, never read it though. It talks about what it takes to become a millionaire?"

"Pretty much. The interesting thing though is that the authors summarize findings from their research into the key characteristics that explain how wealthy individuals - defined as those with a net worth of at least $1 million - became wealthy. As you might expect, their results reveal qualities of this group that stand in stark contrast to the earn-and-burn, or earn-and-consume behaviors, as I like to say, embraced by most. The wealthy folks they talk about in the book employ principles such as wisely choosing their professions, eschewing conspicuous consumption, living below their means and being proficient in targeting marketing opportunities."

"Sounds about right to me," said Charles.

"The authors make clear that anyone can become wealthy, provided they are disciplined in their approach and determined to persist in their efforts."

"I would agree with that. I would add that developing a plan early in adulthood, avoiding debt, particularly credit card debt associated with buying shit you really don't need, and making regular contributions to retirement plans will definitely serve someone well."

"You would get no argument from me, Mr. Bingman."

For nearly two hours the friends remained silent and listened to the comforting voice of the book's narrator. Just as they started to tire of listening to the book, began to lose hope that Morrison would show up, and started focusing on their shift ending, a dark blue sedan pulled slowly into the business center parking lot and proceeded to exit immediately. Unable to contain his mounting frustration, Charles dropped an 'F' bomb. "What the fuck was that! What was that clown doing?"

"I have no idea, Honey," Vallory mumbled. "It could have been anything. Maybe they thought one of the businesses was open today or maybe they were checking the hours of operation. Who knows? They could have pulled in for any number of reasons or for no reason at all. The only thing we know for sure is that it isn't our man Morrison.

Their disappointment and frustration was quickly replaced with excitement as a second dark sedan pulled into the lot a minute or so later.

"Now that looks like an Infiniti," offered Vallory.

"I think you're right, Val."

"That is definitely an Infiniti sedan," Vallory proclaimed. "It looks like one of those new Q50s." Now the friends were wide awake and alert. Pulling near the spot where Vallory had parked twice recently herself, the driver brought the car to a stop. With their eyes trained on the vehicle, for what seemed like an eternity, the friends waited for a door to open ... nothing. The car remained motionless for another two or three minutes. No one got out, no one approached it. Nothing. Finally, after Charles and Vallory were sure the engine would be started and the car would simply drive off, the driver side door opened. Although they knew no one could make out individuals in a car at the distance they were parked, they both reflexively slumped lower in their seats. As the driver exited the car, stood upright and stretched, they whispered in unison, "Morrison."

Morrison looked around briefly as he made his way to the stairs. Moments later he was in his office, at his desk and turning his computer on. While the computer did what it needed to do to wake up, he opened the drawer where he kept his mail. "Helix Real Estate Group, Helix, Helix," he mumbled to himself as he shuffled through the stack of mail. Nothing. *Nothing at all from Helix*, he thought. *Maybe Darlene was mistaken.* Setting the stack of letters on his desk, he turned his attention to his computer. He wanted to check his email while he was here and take a quick look at some of the client accounts. He had promised himself he wouldn't 'borrow' any more money from those accounts; however, he felt compelled to just verify some of the balances in case it became necessary to do so. "You've dug a hole for yourself, Carl, but it's not too deep yet. You can still dig yourself out," he mumbled. *You can still dig yourself out.*

It had been awhile since he logged onto his work computer and for the moment, the password escaped him. "Ahh, here we go," he blurted out as he let his hands hover over the keyboard and typed 'Money4Life!$' and hit the 'Enter' key. Much to his surprise his entry was met with *Incorrect Password.* Assuming he fat fingered it, he typed it again ... much more slowly.

Again his entry was met with *Incorrect Password.* Reaching into the bottom drawer on the right side, he reached toward the back and pulled out the small piece of paper taped there. Glancing at the paper he saw that he was not mistaken. Just as he thought, the bold type on the paper confirmed his password was 'Money4Life!$.' Pecking away at the keyboard with his right forefinger, deliberately selecting each character, he entered 'Money4Life!$' one more time ... *Incorrect Password. Your Account Has Been Locked.* "Fuck!" he yelled out as he smacked the keyboard. "What else could go wrong?" he said to the ceiling as if an answer from upstairs might be forthcoming. *Oh well, I'll just have to use Outlook Web Access from the house later*, he thought to himself. "Fuck! What else could go wrong?" he asked the room.

"What do you think is going on up there?" asked Vallory.

"I don't know for certain what's going on up there, but I do know what I hope is going on," said Charles. "There are two things we are counting on. One, Morrison finds the letter from the Helix Real Estate Group; and two, if Paul is the computer guru we need him to be, Morrison gets locked out of his computer should he try to logon. The last thing we need is for him to access information related to professional contacts, like Malone, and perhaps just as importantly, to have continued access to client's money. History is replete with desperate people throwing caution to the wind when they feel their backs are to the wall."

With computer access, the initial access required for further access to his email and the client accounts, denied, he turned his attention back to the letter Darlene had mentioned. He sometimes left mail or paperwork on top of the filing cabinet. *Maybe it's over there*, he thought, glancing across the room. Rising from his chair, he hadn't taken more than two steps toward the filing cabinet when it became clear that there wasn't anything sitting on top. *Where else might I keep a letter? Only in the desk drawer*, he thought as he returned to his chair. *It's gotta be in this drawer!* Pulling it open a second time, he pulled out the stack of letters and a group of loose papers ... and there it was, an envelope with the return address for 'Helix Real Estate Group' typed neatly in the upper left hand corner. "I really have to do a better job of filing and managing my snail mail," he informed the empty room. Grabbing the letter opener out of the pen and paper cup he kept on the corner of his desk, he anxiously ran it along the top edge, splitting the top seam of the envelope, exposing the letter inside. Raising the envelope toward his mouth, he gave it a forceful blow. Just then the name of the Helix Real Estate Group guy he had talked came to him. *Jordan. Jordan Malone.* Reaching into the envelope he grabbed the letter:

HELIX REAL ESTATE GROUP

September 1, 2014

Jordan P. Malone
President, Business Development
10776 W. Twain Avenue, Suite #332
Las Vegas, NV 89135
(702) 832-2882

Carlton F. Morrison III
CEO, Blackstone Financial Services Group
4160 Paradise Road, Suite #15
Las Vegas, NV 89169
(702) 792-2216

Mr. Morrison,

Our group is in the process of developing multiple commercial properties here in the Las Vegas area. Every indication is that the local market has found a bottom, and in fact, is poised for a significant recovery. Helix Real Estate Group is positioning itself to be on the leading edge of that recovery.

We are currently reaching out to respected, leading financial services companies here in the Las Vegas area to partner with us in this endeavor. Below are the general terms of our Base Proposal:

- Minimum Investment: $2.5M
- Guaranteed Investor Annual Return: 7%
- Term: 60 Months

The Extended Proposal:

- Minimum Investment: $4M
- Guaranteed Investor Annual Return: 8%
- Return from Rents: 3%
- Term: 60 Months

Notes: Payments will be made monthly starting January 15th, 2015. While the rate of return to investors from rents is guaranteed, the projected rents income cannot be guaranteed as it will vary. The current projection is $150,000 monthly.

I hope you give consideration to our proposal and I look forward to hearing from you.

Best Regards,

Jordan P. Malone

For a long time Morrison simply sat there. The slightest of smiles slowly spread across his face as it dawned on him that this might be an answer to his financial woes. Reaching into his pocket he pulled out his phone and opened the compound interest calculator app. He was pretty good at math but there weren't many people that could run these numbers in their head. Both proposals looked interesting but he immediately focused on the Extended Proposal. With all the numbers plugged in he hit 'Enter' and stared at the numbers on the screen. His magic app told him that a $4,000,000 investment would yield a return of $5,877,312.31, which worked out to 60 payments of $97,955.21. Running the numbers for the Rents on a projection of $150,000 monthly, the result was $4,500 monthly. Taken together, he could be looking at returns of $102,455.21 monthly - give or take depending on what happens with the Rents - for the next five years; and a total return of something in the neighborhood of $2,000,000 for a $4,000,000 investment.

While there was a lot to like about the Extended Proposal, two issues immediately popped into his head. "This is a good long-term deal that doesn't really address my short-term problem, the Bank of the West loan. Second, while I have the money, I would rather not part with it," he whispered to himself in the eerily quiet office. *You know*, he thought to himself, *even though I hate to do it, I could take a small loan from some of the client accounts.* As the thought came to him, he immediately reached for his mouse, waking his computer which had drifted off to standby mode. Halfway through typing his password he remembered that he was locked out of his computer. "Fuck, fuck, double fuck!" he yelled at the wall as he slammed his fist on his desk.

"When you have a minute, come give this a look," Dave called out to his wife as he sat staring at the computer screen in their den. "I think it's ready to go he whispered to himself," as he waited for her. Moments later Mary popped into the den and slowly read the email, looking over her husband's right shoulder.

"Looks good to me."

"You sure?"

"Yes, Dave. I read it twice and it looks good."

"Well, here goes nothing," he said as he hit the 'Send' button.

For the next twenty minutes, Carl searched furiously throughout his office. The funny thing was, he knew exactly where the contact information for technical support was on his computer. *Oh the irony*, he thought. *The information I need to have the computer repaired is easily found on the computer denying me access. Oh the bitter irony indeed.* He wouldn't give up though. He knew he had the business card for Desert Computer Technical Services somewhere in his office. In fact, he had stumbled across the card recently when looking for something else. "Isn't that always the case?" he asked himself, "you tend to find things just at the point you aren't looking for them." Finally it dawned on Carl he didn't need to find the card. Not only did he not need to find the number right now, after all, it was Sunday night and he would have to wait until tomorrow to get someone out here; also, he could use his cell phone or his home computer to search for the phone number. He could have kicked himself for the time wasted and the unnecessary frustration. The only issue was avoiding Darlene. As far as she knew, he was supposed to be in Texas for at least a few more days and possibly until a week from tomorrow. He couldn't very well just stroll in here tomorrow as if he hadn't left that message on her phone. "Oh well, I'll come up with something," he apprised his computer monitor as he hit the power switch. Leaving the office the way he had found it, he locked up and headed home.

As he contemplated the situation on the 20 minute ride home, Morrison was thrilled to see that some of the networking he had performed in the past might actually pay dividends at a critical time for him. The difficulty however, was that he was going to have to move on the Extended Proposal quickly. He had already established Wednesday as the drop dead day, the travel day, if he couldn't get this issue resolved. At this point, timing was everything. It wasn't lost on him that even if he took advantage of the Extended Proposal from Helix, while it absolutely helped his long-term prospects, it didn't address his immediate problem, the loan from Bank of the West. Drumming his fingers along the top of the steering wheel, he knew that the bank situation called for an immediate infusion of cash. The only option he could see at this point was to reach out to prospective clients. He had a few in mind; there were a handful that had expressed an interest in BFSG in the past but were not willing at the time to pull the trigger on a six figure investment. His mind was racing, trying to recall the names and situations of different prospects, as he arrived home and pulled into the garage.

Walking through the garage door, Morrison headed straight for the kitchen. He was starving. Unfortunately, a look through the refrigerator revealed there wasn't much to choose from. As he wasn't in the mood to cook anything and he didn't feel like going back out, it looked like his options were leftover lasagna or chili. He decided on the chili. While the bowl of chili warmed in the microwave, he headed to his bedroom, kicked off his shoes and changed into some shorts and a tee-shirt. Sitting on the edge of the bed, he had just started to give more thought to which prospects to hit up when he was snapped out of his reverie by the beeping microwave. "I guess the chili is ready," he muttered to the empty space. Grabbing his dinner, he headed into the living room and flipped on the television. After a full minute of mindlessly tapping the 'channel up' button, he finally settled on TNT which was doing a *Rocky* marathon. At some point, around the time Rocky was involved in a training session with his old nemesis, Apollo Creed, he fell asleep.

When he awoke, the *Rocky* Marathon had ended, replaced by an infomercial for a new high-speed vacuum cleaner. Glancing at the microwave clock in the kitchen he saw that it was 2:36 a.m. The pitchman on television was nearly overcome with emotion when describing how the lightweight, compact vacuum cleaner was designed with the full-sized features of an upright vacuum in a package that is half the size. He went on to celebrate the fact that the new technology harnessed hurricane-like cleaning power with twin motors, one for the brush bar and one for suction. "Wow, who could bypass such a revolutionary product?" Morrison asked himself rhetorically. *What's the old saying?* Morrison thought to himself, *a fool and his money are soon parted?* Bending and grabbing the remote, which had fallen off the couch onto the floor, Morrison turned off the television and headed for his bedroom.

After laying in bed for 20 minutes, it became obvious that he wasn't going to fall back asleep anytime soon. Sitting up in bed, he let his feet fall to the floor and debated whether he should try to find something to watch on television or check email. He decided on the latter. Making his way to the den, he sat down and awoke the computer from sleep mode. He couldn't remember the last time he had used Outlook Web Access, but it was his only option for checking work email until he could schedule technical support to take a look at his office computer. Logging in, he wasn't surprised to see the 92 messages that awaited him; it had been awhile since he checked his mail. He diligently made his way through his inbox, which didn't take too long considering a fair number of the emails were simply bothersome solicitations for which he had no interest. He immediately deleted those. Next, he turned his attention to emails from clients; picking those out quickly by name recognition. Most were mundane requests or questions he was able to address quickly and easily. A few would require more nuanced answers, so he simply dismissed those for the moment, planning to answer later. One of the last emails was neither a solicitation nor a name he immediately recognized; although there was a sense of familiarity. "So, what business do you have Mr. Welles?" he mumbled through a yawn as he double-clicked the email.

From: Welles, David J. Sent: Sun 10/05/2014 6:18 PM
To: FJMorrison@BFSG.com
Cc:
Subject: Investment Opportunities

Greetings Mr. Morrison,

I hope you are well. You may not remember, but we spoke about three years ago in regard to investment opportunities for accredited investors. While I was on the cusp, unfortunately, I did not meet the income requirement of $200,000 per year at that time.

I am reaching out to you today because thanks in part to a recent marriage, my wife and I meet the 'accredited investor' joint income requirement of $300,000. In fact, we now meet either requirement for accredited investor status as the recent run up in the stock market has pushed our net worth to $1.2 million.

My wife and I have been reviewing our portfolio and determined that we would like to diversify our holdings and put some money to work with a financial services company that can offer a more hands-on, personalized service. At this time we are prepared to move half of our portfolio, $600,000, to such a firm.

During the course of discussions with my wife, I was reminded of my conversation with you and the services provided by Blackstone Financial Services Group; and my wife suggested that I reach out to you. We are preparing to depart for a trip to Europe on October 8th and were hoping to meet with you to discuss potential investment opportunities before that time.

I look forward to hearing from you.

David J. Welles

Sitting there, slightly dumbfounded by this apparent good fortune and feeling a little loopy, probably because of simple fatigue, he couldn't repress the smile that spread across his face and the thought that popped into his head, *you're going to be alright Carl, things always have a way of working out for you.*

[9] THE BUILD-UP

Monday morning. "Today is the 6th," Morrison verified with himself, glancing at the lower right hand corner of the computer's taskbar. "That doesn't leave a lot of time." While he couldn't pin down the name David J. Welles precisely, he couldn't shake the feeling that there was something familiar about it. Maybe he had met him at the Lifestyle and Retirement Symposium, a terrific event - hosted annually by The National Association of Personal Finance Professionals - that provided a unique opportunity for potential clients to speak with financial planners and voice their concerns with how planners provide financial services. He attended the event each year not only because it offered a chance to meet potential clients, but because it was a great way to network with other financial professionals and learn more tricks of the trade. *I'll give Welles a call later this morning,* he thought. *I absolutely need to touch bases with him before Wednesday.* He had to stifle a yawn as he reached for the power button, turning off the monitor. Making his way back to the bedroom, he climbed back into bed and was fast asleep within minutes.

Unbeknownst to the group, the subject of their conversation was dead to the world 18 miles away, splayed out on his bed and snoring quite loudly after a late night, as they enjoyed breakfast at Buckman's Grille. "Although we've eaten lunch as a group here a few times, I believe this is the first time we've all been her for breakfast," said Vallory.

"I believe you are correct, Val," Chad said, "that's hard to believe when you consider how often most of us eat here."

"I don't think the breakfast menu is as good as the lunch menu but the views of the valley and strip are incredible. It's a great way to start a relaxing day and it always seems like there is a hummingbird that flies along the flower bed underneath the window every time Dave and I are here," said Mary. Her husband nodded in agreement. "Great, great views," he said, "absolutely can't be beat."

"So, where are we with Morrison, Charles?" Bill asked.

"Well, you and Dave need to be standing by. My guess is that he will reach out to one or both of you today, considering time is a factor with both deals. We have to assume he has the Helix letter and 'David J. Welles' has contacted him via email, correct Dave?"

"Indeed. Indeed he has," said Dave, smiling as he took a sip of his coffee ... which had grown cold. Raising his hand slightly, he just missed catching the eye of their waiter who disappeared into the kitchen. *Oh well*, he thought, *I'm sure he'll be by this way soon enough.*

"For what it's worth, with the weekend out of the way, we have updated the voicemail on our disposable pre-paid," said Bill.

"You guys want to hear?" asked Chad.

"Sure," said Sandra.

"Let's hear how professional you guys can sound," said Vallory.

"Someone give me a call at (702) 832-2882," instructed Bill.

Reaching her phone first, Mary did just that. Placing his phone in the middle of the table, Bill hit the speaker button. After four rings, Bill's familiar voice sprang from the phone:

> "You have reached Jordan Malone with the Helix Real Estate Group, the premiere real estate services company in Southern Nevada for more than 30 years. I am unable to take your call right now, but if you will kindly leave your name, number and a short message, I will return your call as soon as I'm able. Thank you."

"Wow, very nice," said Sandra. "That sounded perfect."

"Why thank you, Sandra."

"What can we ... or what should we be doing at this point?" asked Vallory as she turned to look at Charles.

"If Morris ... when Morrison reacts to the letter and email we proceed with the next phase of the plan as we discussed previously. At this point we have to show patience and restraint; and let him come to us," Charles said authoritatively. "These next two days will likely be two of the longest of our lives."

"Patience, patience, patience," said Sandra.

"Excuse me," said their waiter, appearing out of nowhere. "Can I get you folks anything else this morning?"

"A little more coffee for me," Dave indicated.

"Anyone else?" Sandra, Charles and Vallory nodded in the affirmative.

"I've got a fresh pot in the kitchen. I'll be right back." As they waited for his return, the group reflected on what might happen if their money was lost.

"Quite honestly, I'm terrified of being financially ruined," offered Sandra. You see documentaries, or read, about the Stock Market Crash of 1929, the dot-com bubble of 2000, or the financial crisis we just went through a few years ago and the hell that was wrought on people and you never imagine that could be you. Until now, losing everything has never felt like such an existential threat."

"It's scary how quickly things can change," said Chad.

"Agreed," said Bill, looking at his partner.

"No doubt this situation has the ability to go way beyond a financial setback. When I think of a setback, I think of something that presents difficulties and results in some short-term changes. The setback might be the result of a temporary job loss, a reduction in real estate values, a reduction in family income or an extended bear market that drives down stock prices," said Charles. "This is something that has the potential to go way beyond that."

"There is absolutely no doubt that this shit with Morrison could go way beyond that," George seethed as Sandra reached over and grabbed his hand, squeezing gently. "This has the potential to be absolutely ruinous."

"You know, I've never been afraid of hard work and I've always felt like I could put forth increased effort to overcome an obstacle, any obstacle, when necessary," said Vallory.

"I know what you mean," said Charles.

"However," Vallory continued, "while I'm not too old to go back to work, who the hell is going to hire me?"

"I know what you mean ... "

"Here you folks go, a fresh pot of coffee," said the waiter as he returned to the table and poured four cups. "Anything else for now?"

"Nope, that should do it," said Vallory, answering for the group.

"I know what you mean," Dave continued, "I was reading an article not too long ago that highlighted the struggles of some older Americans shut out of the workforce. One guy they talked to, 56 or 57 I believe, had spent thousands of dollars to go back to school to sharpen his technology skills and sent out literally hundreds of resumes, but after two years, he was still unemployed. He only had something like one or two interviews in the previous eight months. It's crazy. Another fifty-something guy found work after about 18 months; however, it was significantly less than what he had made previously and below what one would expect considering his education and formidable experience."

"Exactly!" said Vallory. I read a report from the Department of Labor that said the number of people 45 and older who have been jobless for more than a year has quadrupled since 2007, accounting for nearly half of the 3.5 million Americans out of work for more than a year. The older someone is and the longer they have been out of work, the harder it becomes for them to find work. Their skills atrophy, their network is diminished and they lose connections; and unfortunately, they are viewed by prospective employers as damaged goods ... not worth the time. It turns into a vicious cycle; and even if I found a decent job next month, how long would it take to get myself back to a position financially to retire with a modicum of comfort, less known all the way back to where I was?"

"As much as I hate to think about it," Chad added, "I have given thought to how we would go about moving on if this situation with Morrison and BFSG leads to our financial ruin. First, I believe we will have to accept the reality that we may no longer be able to afford some things we've grown accustomed to without much thought. It will likely mean doing away with non-essential expenses such as vacations, the premium cable package, designer clothes, new cars every three years and eating out as often. Second, we will have to work ourselves back into the workforce. But like George and Val were just saying, that is likely easier said than done. It would be tough competing with a twenty-something for a job. I'm just thankful our house is paid off. The thought of living in my car, or worse, the street, scares the shit out of me."

"Well, let's hope it doesn't come to that," said Charles. Looking to clear the air of all the negative energy and inject some positivity into a group that had grown incredibly dour over the last 15 or 20 minutes, he noted that they had acted quickly and decisively when they suspected something wasn't right and they weren't beaten just yet. Operation Money Recovery was in full effect and he believed it had a reasonable chance for success. They just needed to be on their toes over the next few days, execute precisely and be prepared to carry out their plan at all costs.

Just as Charles looked around and started to raise his hand to get the waiter's attention, he made his way to their table. "Anything else for you folks." They each indicated that they were finished.

"Just the checks please," said Charles.

"And how would you folks like those split up?" With the breakdown confirmed, the waiter excused himself, promising a speedy return.

"You're right, Charles. We are doing exactly what we need to be doing and I have to believe that we will be successful," said Vallory. Moments later the waiter returned with four checks. "Thank you and you folks have a fantabulous day."

"Fantabulous?" asked Mary.

"Yes, Ma'am. That's what happens when fantastic collides with fabulous."

"Well alright then," said Mary. "Fantabulous it will be."

"Shit!" Morrison exclaimed as he rolled over and glanced at the bedside clock. 9:16 a.m. He never slept in that late. Throwing his feet over the side and sitting on the edge of the bed, Morrison grabbed the tee-shirt he had worn last night and pulled it over his head. Taking a second to first gather his thoughts, he let out a deep yawn as he rose to his feet and headed toward the den. *Dammit! forgot my phone.* Grabbing the letter, he did a U-turn and headed back to the bedroom. "You've got to be kidding me?" he asked as he stared at the non-responsive phone. Taking a deep breath, and as calmly as possible, he reached into the nightstand drawer, grabbed the power cable, plugging one end into the phone's micro USB slot and bending down, plugging the other end into the outlet. *It's times like this I wish I hadn't got rid of my old school land line*, he thought.

While he waited for his phone to charge, he headed to the kitchen to eat breakfast and brew some of coffee. After wandering aimlessly around the kitchen for a few minutes, he stopped in the middle of the floor with his hands on his hips. Nothing he had in the house, oatmeal, cold cereal or eggs, sounded good. *I think I'll go get something while that damn phone charges.* He had heard about a place that served the best breakfast burritos. It had been a long time since he had a good breakfast burrito. Time might be a factor, however, so he had to hustle. Most places quit serving off the breakfast menu at 10:00 or 10:30. Moving quickly to the den after getting dressed and throwing on some deodorant, he sat at his desk and opened a browser and searched for 'Carlito's Burritos.' Seconds later, the magic search engine spit out the answer he was looking for. *Here we go, Carlito's Burritos, 3345 East Patrick Lane.*

He would email Welles and call Malone, over at Helix Real Estate Group, when he returned. First however, some breakfast. Hustling down to the car, he was on his way a mere eight minutes after deciding to give this new place a try. Settling into what should be a 10 - 12 minute ride, he selected the third favorites button on the radio, NPR, after just a few minutes of the 70s station and even less time with the 80s station. His timing was perfect as he had tuned in just in time for the business and finance news segment:

> Host: "Welcome back. I hope your Monday is off to a great start. Changes at the Social Security Administration. Starting in September, the Administration will resume mailings at five-year intervals to workers who have not signed up to view their statements online through 'my Social Security,' according to an agency spokeswoman. The statements will be sent to workers at ages 25, 30, 35, 40, 45, 50, 55 and 60, she said, adding the agency would continue to promote use of the online statements.

> As some may remember, the SSA stopped mailing most paper statements in 2011 in response to budget pressures, and saved the SSA $70 million annually, about 50 cents per mailed statement.
>
> However, the decision has been a sore point with some critics, who argue the statement provides a valuable annual reminder to workers of what they can expect to get back from payroll taxes in the future. The annual statement includes an estimate of monthly benefits at various claiming ages and for disability claims. It explains how benefits are calculated and displays the worker's history of income subject to Social Security tax.
>
> In other news, oil prices have plummeted almost 10% in the last two days after Saudi Arabia's Oil Minister, Ali Al-Naimi, indicated the Organization of Petroleum Exporting Countries, responsible for about 40 percent of the world's oil supply, will maintain its collective crude output target at 30 million barrels a day after the latest discussions in Vienna. Joining us to discuss this latest development is Harold Sargent with Fleming's Capital Group .... "

He had planned to get the burrito to go. However, once inside, Morrison decided to eat in. A thirty-something waitress ambled over after a few minutes. "Can I get you something to drink, sir?" Brushing off the Spanish he had not used in years, Morrison replied, "sí, un vaso de agua y café por favor."

"Are you ready to order or would you like a few more minutes?"

"Give me a few minutes, please."

"Not a problem, sir. A glass of water and coffee coming right up." Moments later, Maria, based on the name tag, returned with the water and coffee. "Are you ready to order, sir?"

"I am. I'm going to go with the chorizo and egg breakfast burrito and a side of bacon; and please make sure the bacon is nice and crisp, just this side of burnt."

"Will that be it?"

"Yes, it will. Thank you."

The breakfast burrito was every bit as good as he had heard; among the best he had ever eaten. Sitting back with his second cup of coffee he closed his eyes, for just a few moments, and soaked up the warmth of the sun as the plate glass window he sat behind magnified its impact. Glancing at his watch, he didn't realize how much time had slipped away.

"Will there be anything else?" Maria asked, as she pulled up to his table.

"No, señora."

"¿cómo fue su desayuno"

"How was the breakfast? No, how was your breakfast?" Morrison asked, "is that right?"

"Sí."

The burrito and the coffee were perfect; just what I needed. Thank you."

"Great. Well here you go, Honey. We aim to please," she said as she left the check face down on the table. "I can cash you out when you're ready."

"I'm ready now," said Morrison as he pulled a $20 bill out of his wallet.

"I'll be right back with your change."

Moments later, with his change in hand, he left a tip and headed for the exit. *Time to get home and make some phone calls.*

"Buenos días and come back and see us," Maria called out as he walked out the door.

Kicking his shoes off in the front entrance, he quickly made his way to the bathroom; that coffee had worked its way through his system in no time. Back in his bedroom, he was glad to see that his phone was charged. He checked to see if he had any text or voice messages. Nothing. While the Helix proposal was a tremendous opportunity, one he very much wanted to exploit, it was a long-term consideration. It would mean nothing if he didn't address his short-term problem, the Bank of the West loan; and right now, the only potential answer to his short-term problem was Mr. David J. Welles.

With phone in hand, he headed to the den where he fired up the computer as he sat down. First a reply to Welles, a newly minted accredited investor and someone he aimed to make his new best friend in relatively short order; and then a phone call to Jordan Malone over at Helix. Minutes later he was into his email account and reading the email from Welles. He wanted to confirm what Welles was looking for and formulate the best response. Reeling in this fish was priority number one. If he was going to remain here and continue building the business he started 17 years ago, he had to get this right. Cracking his knuckles over the keyboard, he reached out with his right hand, grabbed the mouse and hit the 'Reply' button.

From: FJMorrison@BFSG.com Sent: Mon 10/06/2014 11:03 AM
To: Welles, David J.
Cc:
Subject: Re: Investment Opportunities

David,

Of course I remember you. It is great to hear from you and congratulations on your marriage; and your new status as an accredited investor. I believe you will find that your new status as an accredited investor will open up a tremendous number of opportunities - not previously available - to you.

Your timing is perfect as I have just recently come across a couple investment opportunities that I believe will interest you and meet your diversification needs. Moreover, as a smaller, customer-centric company, I can offer you more nimble management and a hands on approach that puts your needs front and center.

I understand you and the wife will be traveling soon and I'm hopeful you can carve out some time over the next couple of days to discuss potential ways forward. There is a limited time to act on the opportunities I have in mind. I can be reached at (702) 452-2219. I look forward to hearing from you.

Respectfully,

Carlton 'Carl' Morrison

Finished with David J. Welles for the moment, Morrison moved on to Jordan Malone. Dialing the number Malone had provided in the letter, he cleared his throat and focused his mind as he prepared to use his 'this is very serious fuckin' business voice' when Malone picked up ... he never did:

> "You have reached Jordan Malone with the Helix Real Estate Group, the premiere real estate services company in Southern Nevada for more than 30 years. I am unable to take your call right now, but if you will kindly leave your name, number and a short message, I will return your call as soon as I'm able. Thank you."

Though a little disappointed, as he was anxious to get more information from Malone, he understood that there were a number of different reasons why he may not have answered the phone. He might have taken an early lunch, he could be engaged with clients at the moment or he could be in a staff meeting, just to name a few. *Not a problem. I'll keep an eye on my inbox for a reply from Welles and I'll go ahead and make technical support arrangements for my office computer.* After leaving a brief message, Morrison returned his cell phone to the desktop.

"What do you think?" Bill asked as he and Chad sat idly by as the phone rang and then listened to the voicemail message. "I was so tempted to answer it."

"I know, but we have to stick to the plan. We wait an hour and then return his call."

"Yep, we stick with the plan."

Minimizing the email application, Morrison opened a browser and using Bing, conducted a search for 'Desert Computer Technical Services.' Within seconds he had his answer, (702) 475-9800. Picking up his cell phone, he dialed the number. The pleasant voice of a young woman on the other end informed him that her name was Shauna and inquired as to how she could be of service. "Hello, Shauna ... you did say Shauna correct?"

"Yes, sir. How can I be of assistance today?"

"Well, Shauna, I'm having some issues with my computer and I wanted to make arrangements to have one of your technicians come out and take a look at it."

"Not a problem, sir. I can help you with that. Can I have your contract number?"

"You could if I could get to it. The problem is that it appears as if I've locked myself out of my computer."

"Of course, not a problem, sir."

"Please, just Carl."

"Okay, sir ... Carl, not a problem. What's the company name and your position?"

"It is Blackstone Financial Services Group and I'm Carlton F. Morrison III, the CEO."

"Just one moment while I pull up your account information." Ten or twelve seconds of silence passed while Shauna did her thing. "Okay, Carl, I have your information; and you said the problem was that you are locked out of your computer?"

"Correct."

"Is that a laptop or desktop computer, Carl?"

"A desktop."

"Okay, just one second and I'll see what we have available. Okay, it looks as though I can get a technician out to you on Wednesday between 8:00 - 10:00 a.m. Will that be okay?"

"Actually it won't, Shauna. I was hoping to get someone to take a look at it this afternoon or tomorrow morning at the latest. It is important that I get this resolved as soon as possible."

"I apologize, Carl. Unfortunately ... "

"I have important business to attend to, Shauna and I cannot afford to wait until Wednesday."

"Again, I apologize, Carl ... "

"Mr. Morrison."

"I apologize, Mr. Morrison, however, your service contract ... "

"I'm not interested in hearing about my service contract, young lady. Could I speak to a supervisor please?"

"Uh, yes, sir. Just one moment please."

During the 90 seconds it took for the supervisor to come on the line, Carl had to suffer through a terrible instrumental version of Lionel Ritchie's *Hello*. Fortunately, he was saved, from the likely terrible instrumental version of Christopher Cross' *Sailing*, by the supervisor who came on the line just as the song was starting. *I can name that song in three notes*, Morrison thought.

"This is Ms. Williams, how can I assist you, Mr. Morris?"

"That's Morrison," he replied, even more sternly than he intended.

"My apologies, Mr. Morrison. How can I assist you?"

"As I explained to your associate, uh, Shauna, I need to get someone out here this afternoon, or tomorrow morning at the latest, to look at my computer. It's very important."

"I understand, Mr. Morrison; however, all of our technicians are busy today and no openings currently exist for tomorrow morning. In fact, there currently are not any openings for tomorrow morning or afternoon. In reviewing your service contract, I see that you are signed up for our Premiere service which guarantees service within 48 hours of notification."

"Forty-eight hours? What is required for more prompt service? say something within the 24 hour range?"

"We do offer the Executive and Platinum services which guarantee responses within eight and twenty-four hours respectively."

"Great. Not a problem, just switch me over to the Executive service."

"I will be glad to do that, Mr. Morrison; however, it will not go into effect with respect to this service call. As I stated previously, we do not currently ... "

"Forget it!" Morrison screamed into her ear as he hung up the phone. "Bitch!" Sitting there for the next 10 minutes, he did his best to try and relax, bring his blood pressure down and think about the next move.

If he did need, or want, to drop by the office today, he wanted to be certain that Darlene wouldn't be there. *How can I get her out of the office?* he thought. Sitting there, he drummed his fingers along the desktop and gave it some thought. He finally settled on telling her that he had decided to take this entire week off, not returning until the following Monday, and she should do the same ... with pay of course. What he wouldn't share with her, as much as he liked her and appreciated her years of service, was the fact that he might not be in next week or ever again. Everything depended on what happened over the course of the next two days. Picking up his cell phone, he dialed the office. He nearly dropped it when he heard the familiar tone and message of a phone line that had been disconnected. It suddenly dawned on him that he had forgot to pay the bill. *Shit! This is just the type of thing that could sink me. How would it look if Malone, Welles or anyone in fact, tried to call and that is what they got? I need to take care of this now.*

Grabbing his mouse, he roused the computer from standby, immediately clicked the address bar and typed verizon.com and hit 'Enter.' On the home screen he clicked on the Small Business image and quickly typed in his user ID ... and then he sat there. *Not again. What is the password?* He couldn't believe it, his mind had gone completely blank. He couldn't recall his password. Taking a deep breath, he leaned back in his chair and closed his eyes. Moments later the password came to him and he calmly typed it in. Success! Two minutes later the balance was paid and he logged out. One minute after that he dialed the office number again and was met by his own voice and the familiar voicemail greeting. Following the beep, he left his message:

> "Good morning, Darlene. I have decided to go ahead and take this entire week off. I will be back in the office next Monday, one week from today. Things are kind of slow right now, so please, why don't you do the same. Take the week off - with pay of course - and enjoy some time with Bob. Take care and I will see you next week."

As soon as he hung up, it occurred to him that he should probably try to reach out to Darlene on her cell phone. He wanted to be absolutely sure she stayed away from the office this week at all costs. With his cell phone still in hand, he dialed Darlene's cell number. *Please, oh please let it go to voicemail*, he thought. He really wasn't in a mood, nor did he have the time, to speak with her. After the fourth ring, the greeting on his administrative assistant's phone invited him to leave a message. With the message he had just left on the office voicemail fresh is his head, he simply repeated himself.

Okay, that's out of the way. What's next? At this point, he figured there wasn't a lot to do. He had already replied to the email from Welles and he had left a message for Malone. Now he just had to wait. *Hold on, did Welles provide a phone number? I could try to call him.* Clicking on the email he had minimized earlier, he saw that Welles didn't provide a phone number. He would simply have to wait. His head was killing him. Launching himself out of the chair, he made his way to the bathroom where he grabbed two aspirin. Aspirin in one hand and slowly rubbing his right temple with the other, he walked to the kitchen where he grabbed a glass of water.

Back in the den, he just sat there and stared at the screen for a few minutes. He was starting to feel anxious as there wasn't a lot he could do at this point. Following brief visits to Bloomberg.com and some of his favorite news sites to get caught up on what was happening in the world of business and finance, he rose from the chair again and headed back toward his bedroom, cell phone in hand. After turning the phone's volume to the maximum level he set it down on the nightstand. *My head is killing me, I think I'll just lay here for a few minutes.*

The maxed out volume and the noise that resulted from the phone vibrating on the nightstand woke Morrison from his brief slumber. Collecting his thoughts for just a second, he reached over, grabbed the phone and hit the 'Answer' button. "This is Carl Morrison."

"Mr. Morrison, this is Jordan Malone with the Helix Real Estate Group. Sorry I missed your call earlier. How are you today?" If Morrison wasn't quite fully aware a moment ago, after just waking up, that wasn't the case now; he was wide awake and focused like a laser. "Mr. Malone ... "

"Please, call me Jordan."

"Jordan, I did receive your letter and as I noted in the message I left earlier today, I am interested in the Extended Proposal; it sounds like quite an investment opportunity."

[10] THE INVESTMENTS

Morrison would have reached around and patted himself squarely on the back if he could. The Helix proposal struck him as a solid investment and there was no reason he couldn't close the deal tomorrow. However, he wanted to bring Welles on as an investor before he did anything else. Getting Welles on board was priority number one. Hopefully he would call or respond via email today. The sooner the better. Time was absolutely of the essence. Making his way back to the den after his conversation with Malone, he noticed that he had a new message in his inbox. *Please let it be from Welles*, he thought. Double-clicking on 'Inbox' he immediately saw that it wasn't. *Dammit!*

Tuesday morning. Stepping out their front door, Dave and Mary immediately broke into a slow jog, having stretched briefly inside the house. Heading down Hampton Road they planned to stick to their usual route, making a left on Anthem Parkway and heading toward Sun City Anthem Drive, completing their 3½ mile loop. "I see Morrison replied to your email."

"Yep," said Dave. "It appears as if the hook has been set, now we just have to reel this fucker in."

"So what's the next step?"

"Well, I need to reply and I know we want to wait until later in the day, giving Morrison time to act, but not too much time. What I'm not sure about is whether it makes more sense to reply via email or a phone call since he provided his phone number."

"What are you thinking? Reach out to Charles or the group as a whole?"

"Probably no need to get feedback from the entire group. I'll call Charles after we get back and have had a chance to eat and clean up."

"Sounds good to me," said Mary as they turned left on Sun City Anthem Drive. Finishing up their run 13 minutes later, they slowed to a walk, enjoying the slight breeze while they cooled down. "You know," Mary said, "I have never had a bad workout nor regretted one. While some workouts are better than others, ultimately they are all good and I'm always glad that I put forth the effort."

"So true. I never thought of it quite that way."

After enjoying their breakfast of steel-cut oatmeal, scrambled eggs and some fresh fruit, Dave made his way to their bedroom to take a shower.

"No coffee?" Mary called after him.

"I'll have a cup once I'm cleaned up," he called back.

"Want some company?" Mary asked. "You know, we should be doing our part to conserve a little water. Waste not, want not. After all, we are living in a desert."

"Absolutely," Dave replied. I would love some company. Got anyone in mind? I was thinking of that one actress ... "

"Very funny," said Sandra, as she walked into the bathroom while disrobing. "You're stuck with me, my man."

"I think I can live with that."

"You'd better."

Following their shower ... and more, Mary made her way back to the kitchen and set about preparing the coffee. Once the coffee was finished brewing she poured two cups and called out to her husband. "Your coffee is ready."

"Can you bring my cup into the den?" came the reply. "I was just reviewing Morrison's email and preparing to call Charles; see what his thoughts are on replying."

Moments later, Mary entered the den and set his coffee on the desk, as Dave picked up his cell phone and dialed Charles. Mary stood by sipping her coffee and watching her husband as he engaged in a brief, but intense, conversation. Moments later he hung up the phone. "So what did Charles think? Email or phone call?"

"We're going to go with a phone call. We have to meet with Morrison and consummate a deal today; and we agreed that a phone call would be more direct and make more sense with respect to the available time. Opening the email from Morrison, Dave's eyes immediately drifted down toward the bottom of the email where Morrison had left his phone number. "Well, here goes nothing," he indicated to Mary as he dialed the number.

After the second ring, Morrison walked over to the breakfast bar, picked up his phone and checked the number. Not recognizing it, he let it ring. *If it's important, they'll leave a message*, he reasoned. Sliding his phone into his pocket, after briefly considering leaving it on the breakfast bar, he ambled back into the living room and lowered himself onto the couch.

Once it became clear that Morrison wouldn't be answering, Dave prepared himself to leave a message, which he did when prompted:

> "This is David Welles. Great to hear from you, Mr.

> Morrison. If you are available later today, my wife, Sera, and I would love to meet with you and discuss investment opportunities that might be available with BFSG. I can be reached at (702) 452-8935. I look forward to hearing from you. Take care."

"Sarah?" Mary asked.

"Yeah, Sera. You like it? It's a character from some movie I saw years ago. Sera, S-E-R-A, Sera."

"My goodness, you're really getting into this cloak and dagger ninja shit aren't you?"

"Hey, there is a lot of money at stake for our friends. We have to sell Morrison on both deals. Just doing my small … " Before he could finish, his phone rang. "It's him," Dave said, taking a deep breath as he looked up at his wife.

"Well, you're on David Jules Welles. Do your thing."

"This is David."

"David. Carlton, Carl Morrison here. How are you? Sorry I just missed your call. I was just finishing up with a client."

"Not a problem, Carl. Thanks for taking the time to call me back."

"I got your email and I understand that you, or I should say you and your wife, are now accredited investors and you're looking to make some changes to your portfolio."

"Exactly. I was telling Sera about our conversation … "

"Was that at the Lifestyle and Retirement Symposium?"

"Exactly," Dave said as he looked at Mary, whispering 'Lifestyle and Retirement Symposium' and switched places with her; he stood as she took the seat in front of the computer. Seconds later they stared at the monitor as Mary typed furiously and images from the Lifestyle and Retirement Symposium home page slowly filled the screen. Dave gave a thumbs-up to Mary as he continued.

"I was telling Sera about our conversation at the Lifestyle and Retirement Symposium in 2011 or 2012 … "

"It must have been 2011, I don't recall attending in 2012."

"I believe you are right. I think it was 2011. I was telling Sera about meeting you and our conversation and she suggested that I reach out to you now."

"Great. Well I'm glad she did. Are the two of you available today? I can certainly take some time to meet with you."

"Well, our schedule is kind of tight as we have some things to take care of before we leave … "

"Europe, correct?"

"Yep."

"So where will your travels take you?"

"We're planning on England, France, Italy and perhaps Spain."

"Sounds great. First time to Europe?"

"No, we try to make it over every two to three years. There is so much to do and so many great sites to see; an incredible history. We always have a tremendous time."

"Fantastic," said Morrison.

"We have some things to take care of before we depart but I believe we can make it to your office about 1:00, maybe 1:30."

"That works for me. Let's say 1:30?"

"That sounds good, Carl. We'll see you then."

"Sounds good, David. I look forward to seeing you again and meeting your wife."

Slipping the phone into his pocket, Morrison walked into the kitchen to prepare some lunch. He had considered stopping somewhere and grabbing a bite before heading to the office to meet the Welles but decided against it. *I'm sure there is something here that will sustain me.* Rummaging through the refrigerator, he settled on a sandwich, pulling out the thin sliced turkey, some provolone cheese, some light mayonnaise, a little baby spinach and a tomato. Finishing up the construction of his sandwich, Morrison made his way to the pantry where he returned the bread and pulled out the sour cream and onion potato chips. The final piece to the lunch puzzle was filling his lowball glass with a little whiskey. He wanted just a little something to take the edge off.

The little snack hit the spot. Setting the dirty dishes in the sink, he felt his phone vibrate before it rang for the first time. He immediately recognized the number as Malone's over at the Helix Real Estate Group. While he wanted to speak with Malone today, to close the deal, now was not the time. His focus was squarely on Welles; bag Welles first and then consummate the deal with Malone. These things had to happen in a specific order. He let the ringing phone go to voicemail:

> "Carl, Jordan Malone here. Great speaking with you yesterday. I wanted to touch bases today to let you know that the timelines have moved up slightly. I just got out of a meeting with senior management 20 minutes ago and it looks like we are close to meeting our goal with respect to the number of investors and the required capital. It looks like we're going to close the window on the Extended

> Proposal at noon tomorrow. If you want to commit to this proposal we probably need to get the paperwork done this evening. I look forward to hearing from you."

Morrison's brow furrowed as he stared at the phone while the message played. Just to be certain he didn't miss something, he played it again. *Well that certainly throws a wrench in things. I really wanted to deal with Welles first.* Glancing at the clock on the microwave, he noted that it was straight up 12 noon. He had an hour and half before he had to meet the Welles' and 24 hours, maximum, before he had to get in on the Helix deal. *So much to do, so little time*, he thought. Quickly washing the dishes, he dried his hands and made his way to the bedroom to take a shower and get ready.

Approaching his office, Morrison used his right thumb to turn down the radio's volume on the steering wheel. While he normally would have turned it up while *Deacon Blues* was playing, he wanted to turn his full attention to the parking lot. Checking his rearview mirror, he noted that there weren't any cars directly behind him. Slowing slightly as he drove by, he thoroughly scanned the area for any sign of Darlene's white PT Cruiser. Satisfied she heeded his suggestion and took the week off, he sped up slightly, making his way into the left hand lane and prepared to make a U-turn in ¼ mile. Circling back around, he pulled into the parking lot and quickly pulled into the least conspicuous spot available. Glancing at the clock on the dash before he killed the engine, he saw that he had about 15 minutes before Welles and his wife were scheduled to arrive. Feeling a fresh burst of energy, he bounded up the stairs and let himself into his office, turning on the lights in the lobby area and then those in his office, humming *Love Rollercoaster* the entire time. *Who sang that?* he thought. The first thought that came to his mind was The O'Jays. *Nah*, he told himself, *The Ohio Players. Yeah, it was the Ohio Players. Great song.* He just couldn't shake that song from his head.

The Welles' arrived right on time. "Good to see you again," Morrison's voice thundered as Dave and Mary made their way through the open door and into the lobby area of the office. "Come on in," Morrison encouraged them as he gestured toward his office door. *Good to see you again … for the first time*, Dave thought, but said, "great to see you again, Carl; thanks for taking the time to see us."

"Not a problem. Hopefully I can find a way to help you and Sarah ... it is Sarah, correct?"

"Yes, Sera, S-E-R-A," answered Dave.

With his back to her, and his attention focused on Dave, Morrison couldn't see the rolled eyes. However, Dave could, and he simply flashed the slightest of smiles and gave his wife a knowing wink.

"That's a different spelling. Interesting," said Morrison. "As I was saying, hopefully I can find a way to help you two meet your financial goals. Have a seat. Can I get either of you a cup of coffee or some water perhaps?"

"Coffee sounds good," said Dave. "Thanks."

"Just water for me," said Mary.

"Sounds good. Give me just a minute to get a pot going." Excusing himself, Morrison exited the office and made his way to the kitchenette which contained the coffee maker, as well as a small sink, a microwave oven and a 3-gallon water cooler. *Hell, I hope we have some coffee*, thought Morrison. *I should have checked before I made the offer.* Opening the cupboard above the sink, he saw that they did. After adding the grounds and water to the maker, he flipped the switch to on. While the coffee brewed, he grabbed a Styrofoam cup and filled it with water.

"Here you go, Sera," Morrison said as he made his way back into his office and offered the cup of water.

"Thank you."

"Not a problem. That coffee will be just a minute, David. Cream, sugar or both?"

"Just a little cream." Circling around to the backside of his desk, Morrison took a seat. Reaching into a drawer to his left, he pulled out a pad of paper, a pen and a pencil. "You'll have to excuse me, my computer is acting up and I can't get it serviced until tomorrow. I'll have to go old school."

"Old school works for me," said Dave.

"How about we just get some basic personal information – name, address and phone numbers – while that coffee finishes brewing."

"Sounds good," said Dave. Ten minutes later, after making note of the Welles' personal information and some small talk about the weather, touring Europe and the Runnin' Rebels basketball team, Morrison excused himself. "I'll be right back, folks, let me go grab the coffee for you, David."

"Are you ready, David?" Mary whispered to her husband as Morrison disappeared out the door and around the corner. "Absolutely. How about you, Sera?"

"Ready as I need to be I suppose." Minutes later Morrison reappeared with a mug of coffee. "Here you go, David. One hot cup of coffee with a little cream. I hope you like hazelnut. We are out of the half and half and all I could find was a few little cups of the hazelnut."

"That's fine, Carl. Actually, I love hazelnut."

You lie like a rug Dave, Mary thought as a slight smile spread across her face. *You hate hazelnut!*

"Perfect," said Morrison. "Let's get started. You had noted in your email that while you were on the cusp of being an accredited investor when we last spoke, you didn't quite meet the requirement. Through some good fortune in the market and a new marriage, you now meet that requirement."

"Yep," said Dave, nodding affirmatively.

"By the way, congratulations to the both of you on your marriage," said Morrison, offering Mary his cheesiest smile.

"Thank you," Dave and Mary replied in unison.

"So now your portfolio has cracked $1.5 million and … "

"That's $1.2," said Dave, correcting him. "But we're certainly hoping you can push us past $1.5 million and beyond."

"Absolutely!" exclaimed Morrison. "So you're at $1.2 million and you are looking to diversify by putting up to half of that to work with a financial services company that can offer a more hands-on, personalized service. Have I got that right?"

"Exactly. We're hoping you can put $500,000 - $600,000 to work for us in such a way as to protect the principal and provide some income in retirement."

"I do believe you two have come to the right place. As a smaller financial services company we can offer you more personalized service to meet your specific goals. We eschew a 'one size fits all' approach. I have a couple ideas of how I might put your money to work. "Do you currently have any exposure to real estate?"

"We don't," replied Dave. "Do you have something specific in mind?"

"In fact I do. As you are probably aware, the Vegas housing market is starting to recover and I have recently been in contact with one of the largest, most prestigious real estate firms in the Las Vegas Valley that has conducted research indicating the local market has indeed found a bottom and is poised for a significant recovery. This group is positioning itself to be on the leading edge of that recovery and I have been presented the opportunity to get in on the ground level of a new deal. I'm offering some of my more well-heeled clients the opportunity to participate in this deal which will guarantee a 4% rate of return."

"That sounds great," said Mary. Morrison appreciated the fact that Sera was enthused. However, at this point, he had a hard time gauging her husband's level of enthusiasm.

"It really is a tremendous opportunity, Sera. What do you think, David? Does it sound like something that might work for you?"

"Agreed, it sounds like a pretty good opportunity. Have you closed the deal with this real estate company? Is this something that is already in place and we can expect to start earning returns on right away?"

"Absolutely. In fact, I spoke with my point of contact and sent over the paperwork finalizing the deal just an hour before meeting with you folks."

"It sounds like our timing has been perfect. I'm glad my wife suggested we contact you."

"As am I. So let's go ahead and get that money transferred."

"What about fees?" asked Dave.

"Fees?"

"What will be the cost to us for your services?"

"As a fee-based adviser, my standard rate is 2%. However, because of the level of your investment, I'm willing to reduce my rate to 1.5%. What do you think?"

"The real estate deal sounds great, Carl. However, there is a lot to think about. Can you give us a little time to discuss? Is that okay?"

"Absolutely, David. However, keep in mind that I'm going to have to limit the number of clients I put into this deal so I'm hoping I hear something from you soon."

"I understand, and believe me, we're anxious to reposition our portfolio and lock in a plan before we head to Europe. You should hear something from us later today," said Dave as he stood. Following his lead, Mary and Morrison did the same. Clearly disappointed, but ever the professional, Morrison quickly composed himself and said, "Let me walk you to the door."

"Thanks for taking the time to speak with us, Carl. Like I said, we'll be in touch soon."

"Sounds good."

Pulling out of the Paradise Business Center parking lot, Mary asked her husband what he thought. "Well, of course the deal sounds good, but I think he's lying about closing the deal with the real estate group ... "

"Helix Real Estate Group," Mary confirmed.

"Yeah, Helix Real Estate Group. We'll have to confirm that with Charles and the gang."

"Absolutely. What was the business with the fees? Of course it won't matter since we're not really going to give him any of our money, but that sounds awfully expensive."

"Exactly, a fee-based adviser means that the fee is based on the assets under management. Therefore, as your assets and net worth increase, the adviser gets more. Fee-based advisers can usually also receive commissions for some of the products they get a client to use. In other words, not only would they receive money based on how much the client has invested with them, they can also get a piece of the pie if the client decides to buy other financial products, like mutual funds, through them. My understanding is that while some fee-based advisers offer investors an either-or deal, others might receive payment from both. My guess is that Morrison is the type that seeks to receive payments from both."

"Yikes. What is another option?" asked Mary.

"Well, contrast that with a fee-only adviser. Generally, fee-only financial planners and advisers accept payment directly from their clients. This means that they charge by the hour, the plan, or charge a monthly or yearly retainer; kind of like a lawyer. In fact, the money we have outside of Fidelity is with a financial adviser, J.W. Holloman, a fee-only adviser."

"That sounds like the way to go to me. When Morrison was talking about the fee of 2%, the first thing I thought about was the fact that fee cut the guaranteed return in half. All of a sudden, the 4% looked a lot less appealing."

"Exactly, and that doesn't even account for inflation. If inflation averages 1% a year, and you combine that with the 2% fee, your real rate of return is really only 1%."

"Not exactly a lot to get excited about."

"Nope. Why don't you give Charles a call, have him set up a group meeting this afternoon at our place. We need to let them know what Morrison had to say and determine the next step."

"Will do, Dave. Or should I say, David?"

"David or Jules ... or better yet, D.J. if you please."

[11] THE DOTTED LINE

Tuesday afternoon. "Thanks everyone for getting here on such short notice. Quite a bit has happened since the last time we all got together. I wanted to get everyone up to speed as this thing, good or bad, heads towards a conclusion. Morrison reached out to Darlene ... "

"Yes he did. He encouraged me to take this entire week off."

"He asked Darlene to take the remainder of the week off, which of course, allows him to use the office without fear of running into her. Our friend Morrison has also reached out to Bill and Dave. Why don't you bring us up to date, Bill, on where we are with Jordan Malone and the Helix Real Estate Group deal."

"After a couple rounds of phone tag, we finally spoke and Morrison indicated he did receive the letter, by the way, nicely done Sandra ... "

"Thank you," said Sandra as she exchanged a fist bump, capped off with the optional explosion at the end, with George.

"He did receive the letter and said that he was very interested in the Extended Proposal; as he put it, 'It sounds like quite an investment opportunity.'"

"When did this conversation take place?" asked Chad.

"Yesterday. He thought it sounded like quite an investment opportunity that he wanted to be a part of, however, he just needed some time to get the money together."

"Any idea when that might happen?" asked Charles.

"No. He didn't indicate a specific time, or even a time frame, even though I apprised him that there was a limited time in which the proposal would be on the table. In fact, I followed up with a phone call earlier today and let him know that it was great talking to him and that I just wanted to touch bases to let him know that the timelines had moved up slightly. I told him that I had just recently got out of a meeting with Helix senior management and that we were close to meeting our goal with respect to the number of investors and the required capital. I let him know that we were going to close the window on the Extended Proposal at noon tomorrow. I ended by letting him know that if he was serious, we needed to complete the paperwork by tonight."

"Nicely played," said George. Everyone in the group nodded their head in agreement. "What did he have to say?"

"Unfortunately, I had to leave the message on voicemail; I didn't have a chance to speak directly to him."

"Sounds good," said Charles. We'll have to figure out how we want to follow up if he doesn't reach out to you by, say 5:00 p.m. or so."

"Sounds like a plan," said Bill.

"Any questions for Bill with respect to the Helix deal?" Charles looked around the room and was met by silence; an indication the group was satisfied with the progression.

"What about you, Dave, where are you at?"

"That's David Jules Welles, if you please."

"Oh, my Lord," groaned Mary.

"David Jules Welles? Where did you come up with that name?" asked Vallory.

"Jules was the Samuel L. Jackson character from *Pulp Fiction*, remember him?"

"Of course I do. That's a good bad-ass name. How about the Welles?"

"Orson Welles. I like a lot of his stuff."

"Sounds good."

"So where you at?" Charles asked again.

"As you know, Charles, Mary and I met with him in his office just a little bit ago, hence the reason for calling this little pow wow. Just as a little refresher for everyone, we had noted in the email that through some good fortune in the stock market and a new marriage to 'Sera' here ... " Dave paused just long enough to nod at Mary and witness her eye roll, "I had met the requirement of being an accredited investor. Not only were we looking to diversify by using a smaller, boutique investment firm that could provide more personalized service, we were also looking to diversify our portfolio by putting $500,000 - $600,000 to work in such a way as to protect the principal and provide some income in retirement. Of course he indicated that we had come to the right place, but you'll never guess what he suggested as an investment opportunity."

"Hold on a sec," said Bill, "an accredited investor?"

"I've got this, Dave," said Chad. "It can be kind of complicated, but under federal securities laws, a company or private fund may not offer or sell securities unless the transaction has been registered with the SEC or an exemption from registration is available. Now, certain securities offerings that are exempt from registration may only be offered to, or purchased by, persons who are considered accredited investors. Probably the principal purpose of the accredited investor concept is to identify persons who can bear the economic risk of investing in these unregistered securities."

"I've heard the term, but what exactly does it take to be one of these accredited investors?" asked Vallory.

"An accredited investor includes anyone who earned income that exceeded $200,000, or $300,000 together with a spouse, in each of the prior two years, and reasonably expects the same for the current year, or has a net worth over $1 million, either alone or together with a spouse. On the net worth requirement, that excludes the value of the person's primary residence; and on the income test, the person must satisfy the thresholds for the three years consistently either alone or with a spouse, and cannot, for example, satisfy one year based on individual income and the next two years based on joint income with a spouse."

"Another important point," Charles added, "is that unlike offerings registered with the SEC in which certain information is required to be disclosed, companies and private funds, such as a hedge fund - I'm sure you have heard of those - or venture capital funds, engaging in these exempt offerings do not have to make prescribed disclosures to accredited investors. These offerings, sometimes they are referred to as private placements, involve unique risks and these accredited investors have to realize they could lose their entire investment."

"In other words," Bill said, "you have to have a serious income or net worth to be able to invest in certain unregistered securities and understand that you could lose it all."

"That about sums it up," said Bill.

"Sorry for the interruption," said Bill. "Where were we at?" Bill, who had sat down, returned to his feet and cleared his throat.

"Not a problem, Bill. I was saying that Morrison indicated that Mary and I had come to the right place; and you guys will never guess what he suggested as an investment opportunity."

"Some high speed hedge fund," guessed Vallory.

"Nope."

"Some exotic new commodity," guessed Chad.

"One of those venture funds Chad just mentioned," said Bill.

"Nope. Real estate."

"He mentioned the Helix proposal?" asked Charles.

"He did," replied Dave. "He didn't mention the name Helix specifically, but he did ask if we currently had any exposure to real estate. I replied that we did not. He went on to note the Las Vegas housing market is starting to recover and he had recently been in contact with one of the largest, most prestigious real estate companies in the Las Vegas Valley. This company had conducted research indicating the local market has indeed found a bottom, was poised for a significant recovery and they were positioning themselves to be on the leading edge of that recovery. Your buddy Morrison said he was offering his more well-heeled clients the opportunity to get in on the deal and could guarantee a 4% rate of return."

"Only 4%? Sandra asked incredulously. The Extended Proposal guaranteed 8%.

"What a frickin' weasel," Vallory seethed.

"We indicated that it sounded like an awesome opportunity but that we would need some time to think about it before we transferred any money. So that's where we're at," finished Dave.

"Actually, we concluded the meeting by discussing fees," said Mary.

"You're right," said Dave. "I almost forgot that part."

Mary continued, "Morrison noted that as a fee-based adviser his standard rate is 2%. However, because of the level of our anticipated investment, he was willing to reduce that rate to 1.5%."

"Wow, it sounds as if he is getting a little desperate."

"Or more greedy," suggested George.

"I know he charges me just less than 1%, something like .90%," said Charles."

"Yep, that sounds about right," agreed Vallory. "That is what I believe he charges me." A brief silence fell over the room as the group let all this new information sink in.

"Something else I think you should know," said Darlene.

"What's that?" asked Charles.

"Yesterday, I had to call my girlfriend but I inadvertently hit the speed dial button for the BFSG office; and instead of getting the 'disconnected' tone and message, it went to voicemail as it normally does."

"It appears as Morrison paid his bill and got his phone service back on line," said Vallory."

"Exactly," said Darlene. "Not only that, since the phone service was reinstated, I figured I would check the messages."

"Anything interesting?" asked Bill.

"Well, there were three messages. But don't forget, I don't know if Morrison has checked the messages, and if he has, if he has already deleted some. The first message was pretty generic and not a whole lot to it. A new client wanted to schedule an appointment to discuss his IRA. The other two however, may be a cause for concern. Both were notifying Morrison that they wanted to make withdrawals from their respective accounts, had tried to reach him on more than one occasion and were disappointed that they could not reach him. Actually, Mr. Franklin indicated that he was disappointed and Ms. Ogden, one of his very first clients, said, 'I've been trying to reach you for the last three days with no luck. I hope there's nothing to be concerned about.'"

"Thanks, Darlene. I don't think it's a surprise that other clients are starting to take notice of his absence, and understandably, getting concerned. We suspected as much. That just drives home the point that our window of opportunity is narrowing. It is narrowing quickly. In fact, we need to wrap this thing up in the next 18 hours or so. If we aren't able to get Morrison to bite on the Helix proposal, and transfer the $4 million, we're done. We'll just have to alert the authorities, let them know what we think is going on and hope they can stop him before he boards that plane for Barbados."

"Aruba," said Chad, correcting him.

"Speaking of the money transfer, is the LLC and the bank account set up and ready to go, Chad?"

"They are," said Chad as he picked up a clear plastic binder containing a few pieces of paper from the side table and showed it to the group. "I have all the information for both, including the Articles of Incorporation, right here."

"Was it difficult to get the LLC set up?" asked George.

"Not really. The trickiest part was determining a name that was close to Helix Real Estate Group but not too close. The limited liability company's name must be different from businesses that are already established. I first attempted to use the name 'Helix Real Estate, LLC' but that was deemed too close to an existing business. Ultimately I was able to register 'The Helix Group, LLC.' The registration process involved appointing a registered agent, myself, completing and filing the appropriate forms with the Nevada Secretary of State's office, paying the $232 filing fee and then submitting the List of Managers, each of you. Once all that was done, the Secretary of State's office sent me a certified copy of the Articles of Incorporation."

"So we just have to hope 'The Helix Group' is close enough to 'Helix Real Estate Group' not to raise Morrison's suspicions if we get him to the point where he is ready to invest the $4 million?" asked Bill.

"Yep. When - emphasis on when - we get him to the point of being ready to invest," Charles answered.

"It seems to me that is the least of our problems," Vallory said, "the most difficult thing will be getting him to make that commitment and invest in the first place."

"I agree, Val," Sandra said, "first and foremost, we have got to get him to commit. So where do we go from here? What's the next move?"

"Well, let's see, it's 2:35 now. Bill has already left a message for Morrison and I would suggest we give him until at least 4:00 to return the call. For the time being, I believe we've done all we can with respect to the Helix piece of the puzzle." Turning to Dave, Charles said, "you should contact Morrison and let him know that you and Mary ... Sera, have given it some thought and you are excited about the investment opportunities available as BFSG clients; however, the fee rate is a little steep and you would be more comfortable at around 1%. Of course the rate doesn't really matter since it's not something you will have to really ever have to worry about. However, we do want to add an authentic feel to the back and forth, and if possible, settle your negotiations with Morrison after Bill closes the deal with Helix and we get our money. If we can't push him over the edge on the Helix deal first, we want to settle your deal as late as possible, and as close as possible to closing the Helix deal. Sound reasonable?"

"It does," said Dave.

Grabbing his phone off the kitchen counter, Dave dialed the BFSG office number. Morrison picked up on the second ring, at which point, Dave motioned to the group that he was going to excuse himself and turned to make his way toward their guest bedroom. "Carl, David Welles here ... "

"Every since this nightmare started it seems like I see more television shows and read more stories about financial fraud in one form or another," said Vallory.

"Do you think it is becoming more commonplace?" asked Sandra.

"No, not really. I just think I'm more attuned to the stories because of our situation with Morrison, and of course, the Internet and social media provide more, immediate access to information. Just yesterday I was reading about another case. This one, involving a company called Wellington Financial Group, which involved nearly two thousand victims, seven guilty defendants, $26 million and took place over a twenty year period."

"Good Lord, what happened?" asked Darlene.

"It's what they call advance fee fraud. The bad guys behind this Wellington Financial group convinced its victims that it would either invest in their businesses or find investors for them. The only catch was that the entrepreneurs had to first provide upfront fees of $10,000 to $40,000; and then Wellington Financial Group would do the rest. But as you might guess, Wellington took the money and did nothing, or very little, after that."

"So what did these clients do?" asked George.

"Once the clients began to suspect they were being cheated, and reached out to Wellington, they were told it was their own fault the projects never materialized."

"I'm not that surprised," said George. "Think about it. We are going through a very difficult time economically. When you combine a shaky economy with job insecurity, tighter loan requirements and the need to supplement lower incomes, desperate entrepreneurship is sometimes the result. I've read about other cases like this. As more and more people are trying to make a living and as it gets harder to get traditional small business loans from banks, they to turn to brokers like this Wellington Financial Group. The promise of professional assistance in launching a business can be quite appealing."

"Aren't there laws or regulations governing the behavior of these brokers?" asked Chad.

"Apparently these cases are extremely hard to prosecute. Companies like Wellington skillfully word contracts to make it difficult for victims to sue or for authorities to show fraud. Even if someone wants to sue, the money for court costs and lawyers often outstrips the loss. The other difficulty is that the scam is often hard to spot. According to this story, Wellington ran a first-class website and they had an A-plus rating from the Better Business Bureau."

"That would make it more difficult to spot a scam," offered George.

"Exactly," said Vallory. One of the victims is pushing for federal legislation that would require a broker like Wellington Financial Group to make good on any losses if a client is referred to an investor without adequate research on the company first."

"Hopefully they will have some success in pushing for legislative changes," said Charles. "Financial fraud is definitely a problem, particularly for older Americans. While sitting in my doctor's waiting room the other day, I was reading one of those financial magazines and read an interesting, but not in a good way, article about retirees being targeted by these con artists. The article noted that older Americans are under more financial pressure than ever. Unfortunately, con artists are looking to take advantage of seniors that are desperate to increase their retirement income. As a result, a lot of these seniors end up getting ripped off and losing huge portions of their life savings. The article mentioned a CFP Consumer Guide to Self-Defense which found the story of an 80 year-old woman who attended a free lunch seminar provided by a local insurance agent who gave her a 'free consultation.' This financial professional convinced her to sell her $170,000 bond mutual fund portfolio to buy a 'bonus rate' deferred annuity to reduce the taxation of her Social Security income. Of course, this 'financial professional' scored himself a nice little commission off the deal. They say that retirees are particularly attractive targets for scam artists because, unlike younger potential victims, they often have large amounts of savings available to them. That's why this exploitation comes in so many different flavors."

"And they all taste like shit," noted Vallory, with her unique brand of sarcasm.

"No doubt that there is always someone out there trying to separate you from your money," said Dave, who had made his way back into the room, as he slowly shook his head. "It isn't enough to make the money and develop a plan to draw it down efficiently in retirement, you have to constantly beat back the vultures that are working to steal it from you at every turn."

"Absolutely," agreed Mary. "So, what did our friend Morrison have to say?"

"He delivered a spiel, quite eloquently I might add, that focused on his belief that the fee reflects the value his services provide. He noted that like surgery, his work requires a specialized skill set that benefit his clients; his efforts allow clients to delegate the stressful and complicated wealth management process to a proven professional. He also mentioned that the cost of doing business has risen as the primary expenses related to compliance, rent and technology have increased. He concluded by assuring me that his pricing structure was comparable to that of other financial advisers. When all was said, he apprised me that 1% was not sufficient and he countered with a rate of 1.25%."

"What was your response?" asked Charles.

"I told him I would have to speak to Mar ... Sera. That's where we left it. I told him I would get back with him later this evening."

"Sounds good," said Charles. "When you call back, go ahead and agree to the 1.25%."

"Will do."

"Anyone hungry?" I know it's only 3:35, a little early for dinner, but I assume we're going to be here for at least a little while as we wait to see what happens with Bill and the Helix deal; and with Dave's deal with Morrison."

"I could eat something," said Vallory. "I had a late breakfast but no lunch."

"Same here," said Bill as Chad vigorously nodded his head in agreement.

"We had a late lunch," said Darlene as she glanced at her husband. "Nothing for us. Thanks."

"How about you guys?" asked Mary as she looked over at Sandra and George.

"I could eat a little bit," said Sandra.

"Yep, so could I," added George.

"I could eat a little bit," said Charles. "Did you have anything specific in mind?"

"Not really. I'm open to suggestions."

"The pizza we had last time was pretty good. Plus, it's easy."

"That works for me," said Vallory. "Pizza always sounds good."

"That was from Papa Murphy's wasn't it?" asked Charles.

"Yes it was," said Mary.

"Why don't we just go with that again. If you'll call it in, Mary, we can take up a collection and then your husband and I will go pick them up."

"That works. Same as last time? A gourmet vegetarian, a spicy fennel sausage and an herb chicken Mediterranean?" Looking around the room, Mary noted that most heads were bobbing up and down and no one voiced a dissent. "Alright then, a gourmet vegetarian, a spicy fennel sausage and an herb chicken Mediterranean coming right up."

Pulling her cell phone out of her purse, she dialed the number as she simultaneously grabbed the 'Take 'N' Bake Club' card off the refrigerator. A young woman answered after a couple of rings and then immediately asked Mary to please hold. As she waited for the young woman to come back on the line, she noted she only needed three more stamps for a free 1-topping pizza. *Good stuff*, she thought to herself. Moments later the young woman came back on the line, thanked her for waiting and then proceeded to take her order. "Twenty minutes," Mary called out to Charles and her husband as they collected a few dollars from each of their friends.

Thirty minutes later, with the pizzas in the oven, Mary opened a couple of bottles of red wine while the friends waited. "Well, it's just after four, what do you think, Charles, should I give Morrison a call?" Giving his watch a cursory glance, Charles replied, "yep, now is as good a time as any." Retrieving his phone from the front pocket of his pants, Bill pressed the handset icon as he prepared to dial Morrison. "Wrong phone, Babe," Chad apprised him.

"Shit," Bill said, as he set his phone down on the coffee table and reached into his other pocket, retrieving the pre-paid phone. "Thanks." Sitting back and making himself more comfortable on the couch, he held up his left forefinger, motioning the group to reduce the chatter. Just as he tapped the third number, the phone rang, momentarily confusing him. Glancing over at Chad he whispered, "Morrison."

> Morrison: "Jordan, Carlton Morrison here."
>
> Bill: "Carl, great to hear from. How are you, my friend? I was just getting ready to call you. Perfect timing."
>
> Morrison: "I'm well. I just wanted ... "
>
> Bill: "I'm sorry, Carl. Is it alright if I place you on speakerphone? My assistant just walked in with a stack of paperwork, some of which require my signature."
>
> Morrison: "Not a problem, Jordan."
>
> Bill: "Thanks, my friend."

Setting the phone in the middle of the coffee table, Bill tapped the speakerphone icon as Charles implored the group, by lightly tapping his right forefinger against his lips, to remain quite.

> Morrison: "I completely understand. My administrative assistant and I just waded through a mountain of paperwork ourselves."

Darlene did all she could to stifle a laugh as the rest of the group turned and looked her way. Her husband Bob simply mouthed 'liar.'

> Morrison: "As I started to say, I am absolutely interested in the deal. In fact, I am working to get the funds together even as we speak. However, I don't know if I will be able to get everything in place by tonight. Tomorrow morning is looking much more likely."
>
> Bill: "That's going to be cutting it close, Carl. The window on this deal is really closing quickly."
>
> Morrison: "What would be your guess on the absolute drop dead time tomorrow?"
>
> Bill: "I'm not sure. My guess would be somewhere around 9:30 a.m. Tell ya what, let me place you on hold and reach out to the partner leading this deal and get her thoughts. Just one minute."

Tapping the 'Mute' icon, Bill turned to Charles. "Well, what do you think?"

"You've played it well, Bill. Very well." Everyone in the group nodded their heads in agreement.

"I couldn't remember the time on his flight itinerary to Aruba. Is 9:30 a.m. too late or should I give him more time? Should I press him on making the deal ... on transferring the money?"

"His flight departs McCarran at 12:25 a.m. which means if he's going to run, he'll likely have made his decision and be heading to the airport by 9:45 or so. I would think 10:30 should be good, but might be cutting it close. What does everyone think?" asked Charles. The group quickly acknowledge their agreement with head nods and verbal confirmations. "As far as pushing for the money transfer, I say go for it. By 9:30 tomorrow morning either he will be ready to shit or forced to get off the pot."

"Exactly," said Vallory." Reaching out to the phone, Bill cleared his throat, the room grew quiet, and he tapped the 'Mute' icon.

> Bill: "Sorry about that, Carl. It took me a minute to track down the partner.
>
> Morrison: "Not a problem. Not a problem at all."
>
> Bill: "As I suspected, the window is closing very rapidly. However, I did let her know where we're at and the investment you are prepared to make. She informed me that we could wait until tomorrow. By 9:00 a.m. tomorrow we need a commitment and transfer of monies. How does that sound?"

The group held their collective breath as the other end of the phone went silent for what seemed like five minutes, but was probably only ten or twelve seconds.

> Morrison: "That sounds good, Jordan. Let's plan to meet tomorrow morning to sign the paperwork and close this deal."
>
> Bill: "That sounds good, Carl. I will reach out to you tomorrow morning and we'll put this thing to bed. Have a good night and we'll talk in the morning."
>
> Morrison: "Good night, Jordan."

As soon as Bill tapped the red phone icon to end the call, everyone exhaled completely and exchanged hugs and fist bumps. "Not bad, but we're not home free yet," said Charles. "Let's temper our enthusiasm just a little. We still need to stay focused for the next eighteen hours or so."

Just as the group started milling about and the sounds of three or four separate conversation started to fill the room, Dave's cell phone rang. "Quiet, everyone," he instructed, raising his voice loud enough to command the attention of each one of his friends involved in the various conversations. The group quickly quieted down and returned to their previously held positions in the living room. By the fourth ring the room was as quite as a library two hours after closing time. Taking a deep breath, Dave hit the 'Answer' button.

Dave: "This is David."
Morrison: " David, Carlton Morrison here."

Dave: "Carl, glad to hear from you. I was just speaking with Sera and getting ready to give you a call."

Morrison: "Great. Can I assume that you and the wife have had a chance to discuss the fee rate?"

Dave: "We have and 1.25% is acceptable."

Morrison: "That's great news, David. I'm sure you will find the level and quality of services provided will more than justify the rate."

David: "Well, that's what we're counting on, Carl. Believe me, that's what we're counting on."

Morrison: "Did you and Sera want to stop by this evening and get the paperwork signed and your account funded? I know you will probably be busy tomorrow with traveling and all that goes with it."

David: "That sounds reasonable, but let me confirm with Sera first. Just a minute please."

Morrison: "Not a problem."

Removing the phone from his ear, Dave tapped the 'Mute' icon. "I agreed to the 1.25%."

"Yep, we heard," said Charles. "Sounds good."

"He wants to know if Mary and I can come in tonight to sign the paperwork and fund the account."

"Do you have everything ready?" asked Vallory. "All the bogus personal information you might need for the paperwork?"

"Yep, I think so. I believe we're as ready as we're going to get," Dave said as he stole a glance at his wife who nodded reassuringly.

"We've gone over that stuff a couple of times and both of us know it forwards and backwards," said Mary.

"Well, there you go. It sounds like you're ready to me," said Charles. "Tell him you can be there in 45 minutes." Tapping the 'Mute' icon, Dave returned the phone to his ear.

David: "Carl?"

Morrison: "Yep, I'm here."

David: "Just spoke to M ... Sera and we can be there in 45 minutes. Does that work for you?"

Morrison: "It does. See you folks soon."

"Well, guys, we better get going," Dave informed the group. We need to stop by the house before we head to the BFSG office. Any thoughts before we go?"

"You've done well up to this point, my friend. Just keep doing what you've done. Just stay in character and let Morrison fully believe he has just landed a new $600,000 account," said Chad.

"You guys have done great. Just keep it up," said George, encouraging them both.

Fifty minutes later, Dave and Mary pulled into the Paradise Business Center parking lot. "Well, Sera, are you ready?"

"As ready as I'm going to get, D.J. Welles. "Shall we do this?"

"Indeed. We shall." Three minutes later, Dave and Mary took a collective deep breath as Dave grabbed the outer door to the BFSG office and followed his wife in. Just an over an hour later, after filling out a few pieces of paper and engaging in a banal conversation filled with a lot of fake smiling, Morrison escorted Dave and Mary out of the office, assuring them he would be in touch soon to set up their next appointment and thanking them profusely for their trust in him.

[12] COMEUPPANCE

Wednesday Morning. Morrison had whistled all the way to work. Closing the $600,000 deal with David and Sera Welles last night had been the first ray of sunshine in his otherwise dark and grim reality in a long, long time. The sound of Bill Withers singing *Lovely Day* filled his head. Floating up the stairs to his office he opened the door, letting himself in, and headed back to his office. Lowering himself into his chair, which struck him as abnormally comfortable this morning, he instinctively reached for the mouse, just as he remembered he was locked out. "I wish I hadn't blown up at the ladies at Desert Computer Technical Services," he confided to the empty room. "Things are actually falling into place, it looks like I will be here for awhile and I really need access to my computer. Oh well, I'll have to call later and schedule an appointment. If my luck holds, I won't get that same agent or her supervisor."

Glancing at the clock on the wall, he was surprised to see that it was 7:45 a.m. He had meant to get in a little earlier. He had a number of tasks he wanted, no needed, to accomplish this morning. He was supposed to meet with Jordan Malone from Helix later this morning, he needed to cancel his airline reservations and of course, he needed to make an appointment for a technician from Desert Computer to come out. He wanted to get the Welles account created as soon as possible so he could get their funds transferred and he couldn't do it from his home computer; the necessary applications were only on his work computer. But all that could wait just a little bit. Making his way to the kitchenette, he wanted to take care of the morning's most important event first ... making a strong pot of coffee.

While he waited for the coffee to brew, and welcomed the aroma that had started to fill the room, he hustled back out the office's front door. If he was lucky, Aaron, the accountant from next door, wouldn't be in yet. Walking outside he noticed that the lights in Aaron's office were off, there was no activity and there by the front door was what he had come for; the morning edition of the *Las Vegas Review-Journal*. He preferred the *Las Vegas Business Press*, which did a better job of covering finance, the economy and business news, but he understood that beggars can't be choosers. After taking a quick peek around, as nonchalantly as possible he bent, scooped up the paper and then quickly made his way back to his own office.

As rays from the morning sun made their way to his office through the front door and window, he set down his coffee mug, leaned back in his chair and opened the paper. Thirty minutes later, the paper read - the sections worth reading anyway - and two cups of coffee down, he reached for the phone. The first order of business, he thought to himself, was to give Jordan Malone a call. As he reached for his phone, he heard the familiar tinkle of the small bell perched above the office's front door.

Making his way to the lobby area, he was surprised to see a young man in slacks, a light blue shirt and holding a clipboard, standing there; Craig if the nametag was correct. "Excuse me, sir. I'm Craig with Desert Computer Technical Services." Glancing at the paperwork on his clipboard, he continued, "it appears as if you are having a problem accessing your desktop computer. Is that correct?" Caught off-guard, Morrison was slow to answer. "Sir, you did request a service call, correct?"

"Yes, Craig. I'm sorry. I wasn't expecting you this early ... *or more accurately, at all*, he thought. I'm glad you're here."

"Would you like to show me where the computer in question is located?"

"Certainly. It's just back this way," said Morrison as he led the young technician back to his office.

Twenty minutes later, Craig called Morrison over. "Alright, sir, I'm all finished. If you like, you can go ahead and establish a new password."

"Done already, huh?"

"Yes, sir. If you like, you can enter you new password now." Switching places with Craig at his desk, Morrison sat down and entered a new password. "It looks like you're good to go, sir. Is there anything else I can help you with?"

"No, Craig. That should do it."

"Great," said Craig as he reached for his clipboard, flipped through a few pieces of paper, pulling out the fourth one down. "If you can just sign here on this service ticket I'll be all done and get out of your way." Less than thirty minutes after he had arrived, Craig was done and walking out the front door. *I must be living right*, Morrison thought. *Things are really falling into place nicely.*

Back at his desk, Morrison took a minute to collect his thoughts. *Where was I? Oh yeah, I was going to call Jordan Malone. However, now that I can get into my computer, I think I'll take care of that Welles account first.* Opening the necessary application, he started the process of creating an electronic account for his newest clients. Minutes later, just as he was settling into a nice rhythm, the bell above the front office door sounded for the second time. Rising from his desk, Morrison quickly made his way out of his office and to the lobby area. A well dressed man in a custom tailored suite, perhaps in his late 50s or early 60s, smiled as they made eye contact. Before he had a chance to speak, the stranger raised his right arm and extended his hand as he approached Morrison. "Mr. Morrison I presume? Jordan Malone."

"Jordan? Jordan, I was just preparing to give you a call. What a surprise. A pleasant surprise."

"Let me guess, my assistant didn't get in touch with you?"

"No. I can't say that she did."

"He. I called Todd from the car to let him know that I was going to be stopping by here on the way to work and I asked him to reach out to you."

"Nope, I never did hear from Todd. Not a problem though, please, come on in," Morrison encouraged Malone as he gestured toward his office door. Making their way into his office, he motioned for Malone to have a seat. "Can I get you a cup of coffee or some water?"

"Coffee sounds good," Carl. "Thanks," said Bill as he took off his glasses and set them on the second chair.

"Great, I just put a pot on not too long ago. I'll be right back." Excusing himself, Morrison grabbed his own mug, exited the office and made his way to the kitchenette. Setting his phone down on the counter, he opened the cupboard above the sink and as he grabbed a coffee mug, he noticed that it was a little dusty. Reaching over to the sink, he flipped on the water and quickly rinsed out the mug. Setting the mug down next to the coffee pot, he headed back to his office. "Cream and sugar?" he asked Malone as he peeked his head into his office.

"Both please. Just a little bit of sugar, perhaps ½ a teaspoon please. Thank you." Seven minutes later both men were seated in Morrison's office with hot cups of coffee in front of them.

"So," Morrison started, "it looks like the time has come to conclude this deal."

"Indeed," replied Malone. "Do you have any questions about the terms?"

"Not really. Between the proposal letter and our earlier conversation it seems pretty straight forward. On the Extended Proposal we are looking at a minimum investment of $4 million, which guarantees an annual return of 8% for five years."

"Exactly."

"And the second part of the proposal concerns the rents on investment properties. The rate of return there is 3%, also for five years."

"Exactly. You've got it. While the rate of return on that income is guaranteed, the income itself is unknown though ... "

"The projection is $150,000 monthly, correct?"

"You've got it, Carl. The last thing is that payments are scheduled to begin in mid-January; on the 15th in fact. I hope that works for you and will meet your needs."

"It does. That sounds good."

"Anything else, Carl or are you ready to get started?"

"Let's go ahead and get it done, Jordan. If you're day is looking anything like mine, I'm sure you've got a full slate."

"Indeed I do," said Bill as he opened his briefcase and pulled out a small stack of papers. "I had my office draw up the paperwork for both proposals just in case you thought the Base Proposal would better suit your needs."

"Sounds good, Jordan, but I'm certain the Extended Proposal works better for me and I'm fortunate that I have the money to invest at this time."

"That sounds good, so the Extended Proposal it shall be," said Bill as he returned one stack of papers to his briefcase and set the second stack near the front edge of the desk. "This first one ... " he began as he turned it and slid it across the desk to Morrison.

Fifteen minutes later, with the last document signed, they were ready for the money transfer. "Alright," Bill said, "I've got our bank account information if you're ready to transfer."

"Just a minute, Jordan, if you'll excuse me." Rising from his chair, Morrison grabbed his coffee mug. "Another cup of coffee, my friend?"

"No thank you, I'm good."

"Great, I'll be right back." Making his way into the kitchenette, Morrison closed the door behind him.

Back in Morrison's office, Bill was starting to sweat ... profusely. "Who the hell gets up and grabs another cup of coffee right before closing a multi-million dollar deal?" he whispered to himself. He could feel the moisture collecting in his armpits. *Deep breaths, Bill. Deep breaths*, he encouraged himself. *Everything is cool.* He thought of sending a quick text message to Chad, to let him know how things were going, but after thinking about it for a moment, he had a change of heart and slid the phone back into his pocket.

With the door behind him closed, Morrison approached the large painting, a John Hilton original, opposite the kitchenette sink and lifted it off its hanger, exposing the small wall safe. Slowly turning the safe's tumbler left, right and back to the left - stopping precisely at each number of the combination - he opened it quickly. Following a glance back at the door one last time, he reached in, moved the two stacks of bills - $50,000 in emergency money he liked to keep on hand - to the side and grabbed the paper detailing the Aruba banking information. Setting it down on the small table to his left, he quickly closed the safe, giving the tumbler a quick twirl, and then lifted the painting back into position. With everything back in place, he picked up the paper and made his way out of the kitchenette and back to his office.

Back in his office he moved to the back side of his desk and took a seat. "Decided against the coffee?" Bill asked.

"Excuse me?"

"Your coffee."

"Oh yeah, I had a couple cups before you came and decided I was full. I think I have had enough for one day. At least that is what my bladder is telling me." The two men shared a brief laugh. Taking an imperceptible extended breath, Bill asked, "So are we ready?"

"We are," replied Morrison.

"Alright then, Bill said, "just let me know when you are ready and I will pass along our banking information."

"Just one second," said Morrison as he glanced at the banking information on the sheet in front of him. "I'm logging into my account now." Moments later, barely perceptible, he mumbled "Helix Real Estate Group … "

"Actually, Carl, our parent company is The Helix Group, LLC." Morrison stopped typing and looked up at Bill. "What was that?" Doing all he could to remain calm, cool and collected, Bill smiled and repeated, "our parent company is The Helix Group, LLC." Although Bill was sure it wasn't the case, it seemed as if Morrison simply sat there; sat there and stared at him. As his body temperature started to rise, he was certain he felt a bead of sweat forming just over his left eyebrow, and then …

"The Helix Group, LLC," Morrison repeated. "Got it, and the routing number?"

"Excuse me?" asked Bill, momentarily discombobulated.

"The routing number. Your bank's routing number."

"I'm sorry," said Bill, quickly recovering. "It's 102107519."

"Got it, and the account number?"

"The account number is 319994785634," said Bill, looking down at the paperwork he had brought with him.

"That should do it," said Morrison, lifting his right forefinger high above the keyboard. As he brought his finger down, seemingly in slow motion, Bill realized he was holding his breath. Finally the forefinger made contact with the 'Enter' key on the keyboard. "Done," Morrison exclaimed.

"Sounds good, Carl. Can you please print out a copy of the transfer confirmation so that I can add it to the file?"

"Absolutely. I'll do that now."

"Thanks." Moments later, Morrison rose to his feet. "It's done, I just need to go pick it up off the printer."

"Here you go," said Bill, handing Morrison the small stack of papers he had signed as he passed. "If you like, you can go ahead and make copies for yourself and I'll take the originals with me."

"Sounds good," said Morrison as he took the papers from Bill and headed out to the printer. Four minutes later Morrison returned with two stacks of paper in hand. Handing the one in his left hand to Bill, he made his way around to the back side of his desk. Bill quickly scanned the documents, ensuring that the transfer confirmation was among them … it was.

[13] AFTERGLOW

If either man smoked, they would have enjoyed a cigarette as they both bathed in the afterglow, each certain that they had just closed a great deal. Who was it that said, *"Business is like sex. When it's good, it's very, very good; when it's not so good, it's still good?"* asked Morrison. "Wasn't it jack Welch?"

"I don't believe so," said Bill. "I believe it was George Katona."

"George Cordoba? Never heard of him."

"George Katona. A psychologist, he was among the first to advocate a rapprochement between economics and psychology."

"Hmm," mumbled Morrison, clearly not impressed. Seven minutes later, following a brief discussion of the weather, predictions for what the market might do in the new year, confirmation that each party had a copy of all the relevant documentation and a promise to meet in early January to discuss other investment opportunities, Bill was heading down the stairs and back to his car. He did all he could not to run. Twenty minutes later, he pulled into his driveway where he was met by Charles.

While he hated to part with the $4 million, Morrison was pleased with the terms of the deal. A guaranteed rate of 8% for five years was good stuff; good stuff indeed. With Helix and Malone out of the way, he turned his attention to finishing up building the Welles profile and transferring the money from Welles' current account. Maximizing the clients account application window, which had been minimized when Malone surprised him with his visit, he picked up where he had left off. Twelve minutes later, as he was finishing up, he glanced down at the lower right hand corner of his computer screen and noted the time on the clock in the taskbar, 9:56 a.m.

He was growing hungry, which wasn't a surprise, considering he had yet to eat. Half a glass of juice and a couple cups of coffee does not make a meal. He had a lot to do today, but he figured he could run over to La Casita, a little hole in the wall with great food just a few miles away, and grab a quick bite. Just before leaving, he verified the completeness of the last couple of documents and submitted the electronic packet for the Welles account. *I should have confirmation by the time I get back*, he thought to himself. Walking quickly, he closed and locked the office door behind him and headed down the stairs to his car. Pulling out of the parking lot, he immediately tuned the radio to NPR:

> Host: "The United Kingdom has its own version of Bernie Madoff. A British currency trader has vanished along with

£130 million, just over $203 million, in investors' cash in an alleged fraud that could be one of the biggest in recent British history. Harold Grant, 59, is being investigated by police over the money, which he claimed was in clients' accounts but now no longer exists. In an email sent to clients just over three weeks ago, Grant admitted that his company, The KLM Trading Group, had stopped operating in 2009 after suffering heavy losses on disastrous foreign exchange deals. Authorities report that Grant confessed in the email that he had continued taking people's money for the next six years in an attempt to turn his fortunes around, but all those attempts had failed.

Reports from across the Atlantic note that police have taken statements from a number of victims and begun an investigation. Also, a civil action to freeze his accounts and seize any assets has also been started. The businessman, who traded from an upscale residential address in Istanbul with views over the Bosporus, is understood to have left Turkey some weeks ago. His adult son said he had no idea where his father was. One report suggested he had briefly visited relatives near Manchester and may now be in the Far East.

In his email to clients, Grant wrote: 'Dear investor, I am writing to inform you that KLM Trading is ceasing to carry on business. Contrary to the impression that I have previously given, the business has lost almost all of its assets, and there appears no prospect of those assets being recouped. KLM Trading ceased foreign exchange trading in late 2009 following substantial losses and since that time the business has suffered further losses, which I have tried to make good through investments in a number of commercial real estate projects. However, it is now clear that the business will not be able to recover its losses and must cease trading. This means that, contrary to what was reported to you previously, you cannot expect any payments in the future. I can only apologize unreservedly for any losses or unfulfilled expectations of profit. I have tried to recover the position for a considerable period of time, but it is now clear that I will be unable to do so. I sincerely regret that I have not been able to do better on your behalf.'

> One investment broker, who did not wish to be named, said he had 25 clients involved who had invested a total of £3.2 million and not had a penny back. The broker had begun legal proceedings to have Grant's accounts and assets frozen worldwide. On Facebook, Twitter and other Internet sites, alleged victims have been urged to join the class action suit ... "

Morrison was glad to pull into the La Casita parking lot and end his journey. The story hit a little too close to home; however, he couldn't quite bring himself to turn the channel during the ride to the restaurant. *Fascinating story indeed*, he thought. Taking a seat inside the restaurant, he ordered his meal as soon as the young waitress came over to take his drink order. He was determined to get in, eat quickly and get back to the office. "Just a glass of water, no ice, with a lime or lemon wedge please. And I'm ready to order."

"What will you be having, sir?"

"The enchiladas suizas; and can I substitute the refried beans with black beans?"

"Yes, sir. That's not a problem. Anything else?"

"That should do it, thank you."

Just as he anticipated, the meal was heavenly, even if he did eat it in what had to be a record time. Pulling back into the Paradise Business Center, after pushing the speed limit the entire way and driving a little recklessly, he was pleased to see that it was only 10:48. Not bad. Only about 45 minutes to drive to the restaurant, eat and drive back. Ascending the stairs rapidly, he was a little out of breath by the time he opened the front door and made his way into his office. As he walked past the front part of his desk, he noticed the sunglasses on one of the chairs. Though he was momentarily unsure of where they may have come from, it dawned on him that they must belong to Malone. He didn't recall Craig, the technician from Desert Computer Technical Services, having any glasses. He made a mental note to give him a call soon. First however, he wanted to check the status of the Welles account. It didn't take long. Not only was there an email informing him that the transfer of funds had not been completed, there was a pop-up message in the clients account application, which he had left open, which indicated that some unspecified account information was missing or incorrect.

"There has to be a mistake," he informed the computer monitor. There was no response. Grabbing the paperwork he had filled out last night with David and Sera Welles, he quickly pulled out the page with their account information. *There has to be a mistake, I need to double check these numbers. I must have input them incorrectly.* A careful review of the numbers on the page and those on the monitor revealed that there was no mistake. He had correctly entered all of the information provided by Welles and his wife. *David probably transposed one or two of the account numbers.* I'll give him a call shortly.

Getting up to use the bathroom, he spotted the sunglasses again. *Hell, let me call Malone and let him know he forgot his glasses.* Patting down the front pockets of his pants, he realized he didn't have his phone on him. *Where did I put that thing? Ahh, I think I left it in the kitchenette. Not a problem, I'll go grab it in a minute.* Working his way back around behind his desk he quickly opened a browser and searched for 'Jordan Malone Helix Real Estate Group' as he stood there. He figured he would just find the number and use his office phone to make the call. When the image on the webpage finished loading, he fell back in his chair as if he had been hit in the solar plexus and had the wind knocked out of him.

The face staring back at him, a forty-something, balding black man with a neatly trimmed goatee, was not the same man - a late 50s or early 60s, slightly pudgy white man - that was sitting in this very office not more than one and a half hours ago. Nausea washed over him and he started to perspire as he slowly closed his eyes.

"I have to stop that transaction!" he cried out in the empty room. Reaching into the drawer where he had slipped his Aruba account information after finishing with Malone, or whoever he really was, he was determined to find a phone number and halt the transfer. Within minutes he had found the number and he was on the phone with a Banco Banesco agent. After explaining who he was, giving his account number and the confirmation number; and expressing a desire to nullify the referenced transaction, Morrison waited patiently as the agent placed him on hold. The wait seemed an eternity.

Two minutes later the agent came back on the line, and after apologizing for the brief delay, explained that the transfer had been made through the international banking network and since the recipient's account was registered with the network, the transfer of funds was immediate. Although he heard everything the agent said, he had a difficult time focusing. It was as if he was a dream. "Excuse me, I'm sorry," said Morrison. "What exactly does that mean?"

"I'm sorry sir, what that means is that there is no way to stop or reverse the transaction." The agent continued with his explanation and informed Morrison that his current balance was $1,216,469.04; however, Morrison had already started to tune out the distant voice. His mind racing, trying to escape the fog that had enveloped it, Morrison hung up the phone as he glanced at the clock in the taskbar, 11:13 a.m. He had to plot his next move. Although he was filled with rage and felt a strong desire to lash out at something, anything, he knew he had to remain calm and focused. *Calm and focused is the key.*

"Has the transfer been made?" Vallory asked Charles. "It has," he replied. "As we discussed at the last group meeting, I went ahead and set up a second account. As soon as Bill returned from his meeting with Morrison, with confirmation of the transfer to The Helix Group, LLC, we transferred the money to the second account. We, my friends, are in possession of $4 million. Going back and doing the math, we have calculated that Morrison was controlling $3.63 million that belonged to the eight of us. Tomorrow, a $1,280,009 transfer will be made to my account; $55,600 to Darlene and Bob; $942,693 to Vallory; $756,895 to George and Sandra; and $644,843 to Chad and Bill from the second account. The remainder, $370,000, will be returned anonymously to what I assume will be a court appointed trustee once this all breaks."

"Kind of like in the Madoff case," offered Sandra.

"Exactly," said Charles. "Just so I'm sure, before the transfers are made, is everyone satisfied with the account information they gave me?"

Charles' question was met by a lot of heads nodding in the affirmative. "My guess is that we weren't the only Morrison victims, and when his fraud is exposed, the court will appoint a trustee to distribute any recovered money."

Sitting there, his spirit deflated, he had to accept that the $4 million was gone. Although significantly less, he would have to make do with the remaining $1.2 million. As he sat there in a stupor, he briefly considered contacting David Welles. However, his instincts told him that the routing and account numbers were likely not a mistake or typographical errors. It was much more likely that 'the Welles' were part of this ruse all along; plain and simple, he had been duped. He should have known that the offer from the Helix Group was too good to be true and the timing of getting that significant influx of funds from Welles was too fortuitous.

He had to quickly put this behind him and get his ass out of the country. Fortunately he had got sidetracked and never cancelled his flight to Aruba. Unfortunately, he was going to be hard pressed to make it in time. The taskbar clock revealed that it was now 11:21 and more importantly, it revealed just how difficult it would be to make it to McCarran in time. Going home and packing a bag was out of the question. He had just enough time to leave a quick note for Darlene. She had been a good assistant, sticking with him through those early lean years. Sliding the notepad over and grabbing a pen, he quickly composed a note he hoped would answer some of the questions she was bound to have and secondarily, provide her some cover from an overzealous prosecutor:

Darlene,

I am ashamed to admit that I have committed fraud. I am saddened by the fact that my greatest transgressions have been against those who trusted me the most, you and our clients. Through a scheme of using fake statements I have been able to embezzle millions of dollars from client accounts at Blackstone Financial Services Group. The fraud started nearly twenty months ago and has gone undetected until recently. I was able to conceal my crime of forgery by being the sole individual with access to the multiple bank accounts held by BFSG. No one else in the company ever saw an actual bank statement. The bank statements were always delivered directly to me when they arrived by mail. For my actions I feel constant and intense guilt. I hope you, and our clients, find it in your hearts to one day forgive me.

Carl

Leaving the letter in the middle of her desk, Morrison took one last look around just before he closed and locked the door behind him. He suspected he would never see this office again. Seventeen years was a long time. There were a look of good memories associated with this office; some bad ones as well, but definitely more good memories. Taking the steps two at a time, he quickly reached the parking lot and climbed into his car. Seconds later he was on Paradise Road, racing toward the airport. Halfway to McCarran he yelled out, "shit!," and slammed his fist down on the dash. In his haste, he had forgot to grab the $50,000 emergency money from the safe. *Oh well*, he thought, *what is done is done, I don't have time to go back and get it or to worry about it.*

Seven minutes later he brought his car to a screeching halt at the valet parking area which was immediately adjacent to terminal 1. Time was of the essence, he had no time to park in a remote lot, seek out a spot and fool with parking his car. Moreover, he didn't care what happened to the car after he was gone. As much as he liked the car, it was unlikely that he would ever see it again. As he jogged toward the Delta counter, moving quickly past less time restrained travelers, he reminded himself why he had always wanted to get in better shape. *Getting old is hell. Jesus, it feels like I'm going to have a heart attack!* Reaching the Delta kiosk, he quickly swiped his card and followed the prompts to print his boarding passes. With no bags to claim, he immediately headed to the TSA checkpoint.

As fate would have it, the line was long and did not appear to be moving. Of course that was just the perception of a man under a lot of pressure and in a hurry. Six minutes later he had the pleasure of taking off his shoes, removing his belt and emptying his pockets ... all to no avail of course as the metal detector sounded as he passed through on each of his two attempts. *Somehow I'm not fuckin' surprised*, he thought to himself as the TSA agent groped him while asking if there was anything in his pockets. "No, and that isn't lip balm nor am I happy to see you," was the reply that fell out of his mouth. Stopping briefly, the agent gave him a long, cold stare before moving to his rear to finish the job. A terse, "have a good day," from the agent informed him that he could recover his belt, shoes and the items that were in his pocket. Just as he reached the gate, after redressing and another less than exhilarating jog, the speaker crackled as the gate agent made an announcement:

> "All groups and passengers are welcome to board at gate D23 for flight 2175 to New York's JFK. All groups and all passengers are welcome to board."

Checking his boarding passes, Morrison folded the second one, Delta flight 484 from JFK to Queen Beatrix International Airport, and placed it in his back pocket. Handing his boarding pass to the gate agent, he took a deep breath as the young lady scanned the ticket, flashed her best customer service smile and offered a, "thank you, Mr. Morrison," as he stepped onto the jet bridge. Reaching row 17, he collapsed into his aisle seat. "Four million dollars gone, damn it!" he cursed under his breath. As the plane taxied down the runway and finally took flight, Morrison thought about his next move. He couldn't stay in Aruba long; as an autonomous part of the Kingdom of the Netherlands with whom the United States had an extradition treaty, he had to be prepared to relocate to a country that did not have an extradition treaty in the very near future. He already had a couple in mind and had laid most of the ground work. He only needed to make the final decision on when and where to go.

[14] THE RUN

Monday morning. With some trepidation, Darlene parked her car in the Paradise Business Center lot in the same spot she often did and slowly made her way up the stairs to the office she had been coming to nearly every day for the last 16 years. As she had done so many times before, she reached into her purse, pulled out her keys and let herself in. While she shouldn't have been surprised, the office was exactly like it always was when she arrived first and opened it up; quiet and still. Laughing slightly as she walked toward her desk, she asked herself, "well, what exactly did you expect, silly?" Her eyes were immediately drawn to the letter on her desk.

Setting her purse down on the desk, she eased into her chair and picked up the letter. After reading it for the second time, she set it down, just as she had found it, and leaned back in her chair, closing her eyes for a minute. She had felt a wave of nausea welling up inside of her and she wanted to rest and breathe deeply, just for a moment, to let it pass. She found it hard to believe that her time at BFSG had come to an end, particularly under such horrific circumstances and in such an ignominious manner for Mr. Morrison. Just a few weeks ago she would have told anyone that asked, that she couldn't imagine a reason why she wouldn't be working here for another five to seven years. *My how quickly things change*, she thought. In some ways, she still couldn't believe this was the end. However, she knew this was certainly the end and the time had come to do what the group had discussed. The need to call was even more pronounced seeing how Morrison had left a letter, something that was discussed as a possibility among the group, but not necessarily expected. Taking a deep breath and composing herself, she dialed the number of the Nevada Financial Institutions Division.

Tuesday evening. Following their post dinner coffee, George retrieved the bottle of cognac as Sandra grabbed three snifters. Something of a tradition when they dined together, the three friends often enjoyed a cognac to conclude a meal. George was fond of saying that a good cognac was the perfect digestif. "So what is tonight's selection, George?" Vallory asked.

"Camus Borderies VSOP," George informed Vallory and his wife.

"Is this new or have we had it in the past?" Sandra asked.

"This is new. It comes highly recommended. It's supposed to display aromas of apple, cinnamon, honey and just a hint of peach. Let me know what you guys think."

"Sounds good," said Vallory. As George poured their drinks, the friends muted their conversation and turned their attention to the television, which until this moment, had been serving primarily as background noise. Jim Snyder of KSNV had come on and proclaimed that, "a Las Vegas financial advisor is wanted for questioning by the Nevada Financial Institution Division and local authorities on suspicion of financial fraud and malfeasance."

"Turn that up, would you, George?" Sandra asked her husband. "Unless there is another scoundrel that has been bilking clients out of their hard earned retirement money here in Vegas, I'm going to guess this will be some news on Morrison."

"Indeed," Vallory said, "this should be interesting."

> "Carlton F. Morrison III, founder and CEO of Blackstone Financial Services Group, here in the Las Vegas Valley, is suspected of forging financial documents to steal more than $5.5 million from at least 25 clients, primarily retirees, over a 18 month period. An external hard drive found in a wall safe is among the items from the BFSG offices that has been recovered and taken into evidence."

Early November. "Alright, quiet down," George implored the group. They had gathered at Chad and Bill's to finalize plans for the surprise birthday party for Sandra and Vallory. "We don't have much time," George continued. "They have been gone for almost an hour and my guess is that they will finish up at the Crafts at the Market ... "

"Art at the Market," Mary corrected him. "It's the Art at the Market over at Bruce Trent Park."

"Thank you, Mary. My guess is that they will finish up at the Art at the Market fair within the next hour or so and we really need to wrap this up. I want this birthday party to be a complete surprise. The first thing I wanted to do is confirm the date. We are going with Saturday the 15th."

"That works a lot better than the 22nd," said Dave.

"Agreed, I know that was the day we had originally discussed; however, it turns out we would not be able to get the Bouchon at the Venetian on that day. Also, that is the weekend before Thanksgiving and I figured some people might be preparing to travel then."

"Sounds reasonable," said Mary. "Either day would have worked for us."

"Same here," said Bill.

"Which venue at the Bouchon are you going with, George?" asked Dave. "I understand they have a few different choices."

"Chad and Bill are taking care of the location and menu. I'll let them get us up to speed. Gentlemen, can you fill us in please?"

"Can do, George. We were able to get the Bouchon Patio," said Chad.

"It came down to the Bouchon Patio and the Bocuse," noted Bill.

"Both are great," added Chad ...

"However, we went with the Bouchon because it offers a little more seating and standing room; and it offers a breathtaking outdoor courtyard area," said Bill.

"What's going to be on the menu?" asked Charles.

"Great question, Charles," said Bill. "As you can probably surmise from the name, it's French cuisine and the meal will kick off with some hors-d 'oeuvres, including olives marinées and oefus mimosa; and a salad, maraîchère au chèvre chaud. The … "

"Whoa. Slow down, Bill. All of us don't speak French, amigo. What exactly will we be eating?"

"I'm sorry. Silly me. The olives marinées and oefus mimosa are simply marinated olives and deviled eggs respectively, and the salad is mixed greens, dried herbs and goat cheese with a red wine vinaigrette."

"Thank you, good sir."

"The choices for the main course include: Poulet Roti, which is roasted chicken with Brussels sprouts, fall squash, lardons and chicken juice; Gigot D' Agneau, a roasted leg of lamb with flageolet beans, garlic confit and thyme-scented lamb juice; and Moules aux Poireaux, which is Maine bouchot mussels steamed with white wine, Dijon mustard, leeks and bacon."

"Sounds like some interesting choices," offered George.

"When you receive your invitation - which we will be sending out tomorrow - please, pretty please, ensure that you indicate your selected main course," begged Chad. For those that fail to select a meal, I believe the default will be the Poulet Roti. Also ... "

"That is correct," Bill interjected.

"Also, please ensure that you arrive at least 30 minutes before George arrives with Vallory and Sandra; that means about 5:00 p.m.," said Chad, finishing up.

"The last thing is the … " George started to say.

"I'm sorry, George," said Chad. One more thing. I wanted to mention the dessert. I almost forgot. Dessert will be Mocha Pots de Crème, a rich, pudding-like chocolate, with your choice of a late-harvest Riesling, Black Muscat or Cabernet Sauvignon to wash it down."

"If you want my two cents, and I'm sure you do," Chad said wryly, "go with the Black Muscat. The Mocha Pots de Crème and Black Muscat pair nicely."

"Works for me," said Mary.

"Thanks, Bill and Chad. The final piece is the entertainment. What do you have for us Dave and Mary?"

"Glad that you asked, George. Actually, we just finished booking The Motor City Revue just before we came here tonight. Their tagline is from Hitsville to Soulsville, which should tell you something. They are an 11-piece band covering popular and rare Motown hits, plus Stax artists and popular rock and soul classics. According to the reviews I read, they are authentic and create a very danceable environment. Their website notes that they feature female and male vocalists, keyboards, guitar, bass, drums and a 5-piece horn section," said Mary.

"Love a good horn section," said George. "Although they weren't necessarily Motown acts, I have always loved bands like Earth, Wind & Fire, Tower of Power and Steely Dan with great horn sections."

"That sounds really good," said Bill. "I know both Vallory and Sandra love that old Motown sound."

"So how are you going to ensure they are surprised?" asked Chad.

"It should be pretty straight forward," said George. Each of you should mention, as casually as you can, that you have some plans for that weekend; going out of town, going to see a movie, anything. We want to leave the impression that if we are planning on doing something for their birthdays, it won't be that weekend. Based on past history, they know that we will be doing something. The key to the surprise will be to trip them up with respect to the 'when.' To get them to the Bouchon Patio, I'm going to play it pretty close to the truth. On the Thursday before the party, I'm going to casually offer to take them to dinner at the Venetian on Saturday. I will arrange for the maître d' to escort us to the patio where all the guests will be waiting behind closed doors. As long as none of you, or the other guests, spill the beans beforehand, I believe they will be quite surprised when we walk through that door."

It had truly been a flight from hell. In order to avoid touching down in the United States, he had to take a circuitous route to his destination. The flight from Aruba to Toronto Pearson International wasn't too bad; however, in London he had an airport change - Heathrow to Gatwick - before continuing his journey after a 35 hour layover. After what seemed like a week of flying, the descent to his destination was finally at hand. As he felt the plane start its gradual descent, they encountered some turbulence, and unexpectedly, considering he flew quite frequently, he felt a little nauseous. As the flight attendant keyed the microphone in preparation for an announcement, he closed his eyes and simultaneously took a deep breath, exhaling slowly:

> "Ladies and gentlemen, as you can probably tell, we have started our initial descent into Malé. In preparation for landing, please make sure your seat backs and tray tables are in their full upright positions. Make sure your seat belt is securely fastened and all carry-on luggage is stowed underneath the seat in front of you or in the overhead bins. Please turn off all electronic devices until we are safely parked at the gate. The flight attendants are currently passing through the cabin to pick up any remaining cups or items you wish to discard."

It had come down to Vanuatu and the Republic of the Maldives. Ultimately he had decided on the Maldives because of the lower crime rate, better access to health care, and perhaps most importantly, because of the slightly better exchange rate, particularly since his available funds had been significantly reduced just prior to his relocation to Aruba. He still couldn't believe that he had been separated from his $4 million and left $50,000 in the wall safe. *Well, to be completely honest*, he thought, *it wasn't really my $4 million.* As the plane continued its descent, he watched out the window as Hulhule Island, in the North Malé Atoll, came into view. Mercifully, the plane touched down safely 35 minutes later and his nausea slowly passed. As the plane taxied toward the terminal, Morrison looked out the window at his new home.

Just as he was beginning to doubt the flight crew would properly welcome them to the Maldives, the speaker above his head came to life:

> "Ladies and gentlemen, welcome to Malé where the local time is 4:28 p.m. We will be taxiing for the next few minutes, so please remain seated with your seatbelts fastened until the captain has turned off the seatbelt sign. Your bags can be claimed at carousel two. On behalf of the captain and the entire crew, thank you for choosing to fly with Cathay Pacific today and we hope to see you again on a future flight. Enjoy your stay here in the Maldives. Use of cellular telephones is now permitted."

Reaching into his pocket, he pulled out his cell phone and depressed the power button. As he waited for it to finish its startup routine, he looked out the window and slowly smiled as the terminal came into view. *I'm not sure how long I'll be here, but this place is beautiful*, he thought. According to what he had read, November is the onset of the dry season. He could expect calm sunny days, around 80 degrees with about 80% humidity, coupled with relaxing warm nights. *Perfect.*

> "Flight attendants, please prepare doors for arrival, cross-check and all-call."

Just as everyone was preparing to leave Chad and Bill's, Mary asked, "has anyone heard anything more on Morrison and BFSG?"

"I haven't heard anything," said Chad.

"I haven't seen anything on the local news," Charles said, "however, I did read something, just yesterday in the *Las Vegas Business Press*. It appears as if the Nevada Financial Institution Division has turned the case over to the Securities & Exchange Commission and they filed suit on Tuesday. Apparently the suit alleges that BFSG and Morrison committed fraud by misappropriating and failing to segregate customer funds. The article said the investigation is being led by the FBI's Las Vegas Division. The initial investigation, which I assume involves forensic accounting, has revealed that there has been a shortfall in customer funds dating back to at least July 2013. The BFSG funds, that they have been able to track up to this point have been frozen and will be held in a trust pending the appointment of a trustee who will determine the structure of the payouts to former BFSG clients. The article concluded by noting that the whereabouts of Morrison and the missing funds is currently unknown. However, the authorities have some evidence suggesting that he initially flew to Aruba ... which we knew."

"Hopefully they will track him down soon and make him answer for his actions," said George. As more of the story unfolds, we will get a better idea of what was done and when; and unfortunately, we are likely to learn the extent to which some of his clients ... "

"Victims is more accurate," Mary interjected.

"True," said George. "In the end, many of his clients became victims. My guess is that we are likely to learn the extent to which some of his victims have suffered because of his actions. These cases always seem to end with the revelation that some of the victims have been wiped out financially and end up destitute."

"Surprise!" erupted from the crowd as the doors to the Bouchon Patio swung open, followed by a 'Happy Birthday' serenade from 130 of Vallory and Sandra's closest friends and family. "Wow, so much for a quiet dinner," said Sandra."

"Surprised?" asked George.

"Shocked is probably more accurate," said Vallory.

"But in a good way," added Sandra.

"Absolutely in a good way. You got us, George. I had no idea. None whatsoever!" said Vallory.

"Well that was the idea, my friend." Pointing toward the large table in the front of the room, George guided Vallory and Sandra that way, indicating that was the table for the birthday girls. En route to their own table, they passed by Darlene and Bob who had just seated themselves.

Spotting Paul, who had apparently brought a date, the threesome waived just before they came to a stop at the table Bob and Darlene shared with a couple of Vallory's former coworkers.

"Hey there Phil, Sydney. Great to see you guys," said Vallory, greeting them.

"It's great to be seen. Happy birthday, ladies," said Phil as he raised his glass in a mock toast.

"Thank you," Vallory and Sandra replied.

Following a couple minutes of small talk with Phil and Sydney, Vallory turned her attention to Darlene and Bob.

"Hey there, you two. I'm glad to see you guys here."

"Indeed," said Sandra. I was just thanking them for making it to this little soirée."

"Well we definitely wanted to thank George for thinking of us and extending the invitation. This is great. It looks like quite the turn out."

"Glad you could make. Excuse me, but there are a few of people I want to say hello to before I sit down."

"Not a problem," said Darlene. "So is today your actual birthday?"

"No. Mine is in two days ... "

"And mine is in four," said Vallory.

"Great, well happy birthday, Sandra. Maybe we'll have a chance to talk a little later."

"Sounds good."

As Sandra and George made their way across the room, Vallory hung back. "So how are you guys doing?"

"Hanging in there," said Bob.

"So far I haven't heard a lot about the missing money or Morrison."

"Neither have we," offered Darlene. "I spoke to some folks from the Nevada Financial Institution Division soon after I reported the letter. I left the letter on my desk just as I had found it and spoke to them for about 45 minutes when they stopped by the office to claim the letter and conduct the initial interview later that afternoon. I also spoke to them again ... "

"At our home," Bob said, chiming in.

"Yeah. They came by a few days after that initial visit at the office and asked if I had access to client accounts. I basically explained to them that I took care of administrative tasks such as scheduling appointments, drafting letters, filing paperwork and things along those lines. They didn't stay long at all and I was surprised that they didn't have more questions."

"Do you think they suspect you of anything?"

"No, no. Based on the evidence they have already been able to recover, including the letter, they indicated that they do not believe I was involved."

"Well that's good," offered Vallory.

"Definitely. I haven't heard anything else from them since the SEC filed suit and the FBI took over the investigation, but I suspect at some point someone from the FBI will want to speak to me."

"I suspect you're right. Excuse me while I go mingle. I see some faces I haven't seen in a while ... and to tell you the truth," as she bent down and whispered as Darlene drew closer, "there is more than one I could have gone longer without seeing."

"You're too funny," Darlene said as she tried to stifle a laugh. "Happy birthday again, Vallory and I'm sure we'll talk soon."

"Thank you. You guys enjoy the evening."

"Well, that is certainly the plan, my friend."

Zigzagging her way around the room, Vallory stopped at every table and exchanged a few minutes of chit chat. Sandra was doing the same. As she finally closed in on the main table, where Charles, Dave, Mary, Bill and Chad awaited, she heard the opening notes of *Mercy, Mercy Me.* Turning, she saw the band for the first time. "I was so busy shuffling around and talking, I didn't even see the band. Wow, that singer sounds just like Marvin Gaye. He doesn't look anything like him, but he sure sounds a lot like him. Very nice!"

"That my friend is The Motor City Revue," said Mary.

"Wow, there are enough of them."

"Yep, an 11-piece band covering popular Motown and Stax."

"Very nice. They sound good," said Sandra, who had made it to the table with George.

"Dinner should be served in about five minutes," said Chad.

"So what's on the menu?" asked Vallory.

"We get started with some hors-d 'oeuvres, including marinated olives and deviled eggs; and a mixed greens salad with dried herbs and goat cheese with a red wine vinaigrette," said Chad.

"Mmm ...sounds good."

"Yeah, it really does."

"It better be for what we're paying!" said Bill.

"I hope it was expensive as hell," said Sandra as she exchanged a little fist bump with Vallory. The friends all got a good laugh.

"That's right, because we're worth it, damn it."

Each of the guests had to choose between one of three plates when they RSVP'd," said Bill. "As the guests of honor, you two can choose between one of the three, a roasted chicken with Brussels sprouts, fall squash, lardons and chicken juice; a roasted leg of lamb with flageolet beans, garlic confit and thyme-scented lamb juice; or Maine bouchot mussels steamed with white wine, Dijon mustard, leeks and bacon; or any combination of the three. The chef says it's a lady's choice tonight."

"Nice. All three sound great," said Sandra. "I think I will go with the roasted chicken. How about you, my fellow birthday girl?"

"I believe I will go with the roasted leg of lamb; however, I believe I will have the vegetables that are being served with the roasted chicken."

"Sounds good," said Chad. "I'll pass that word along to the chef."

"By the way, what the hell are lardons?" asked Sandra.

"Related to lard in some way would be my guess," George said, "but I'm not exactly sure to tell you the truth."

"Lardons are small pieces of fat, typically pork fat, that add a distinctly rich, salty flavor. They are used pretty extensively in French cooking," Vallory informed her friend.

"Make sure you guys save room for dessert," said George. "We're having Mocha Pots de Crème with your choice of a Cabernet Sauvignon, a late-harvest Riesling or Black Muscat."

"Sounds divine," said Vallory. Moments later, the food service began.

"I saw you talking to Darlene earlier, Val, what did she have to say? I haven't had a chance to speak to either her or Bob," asked Charles.

"It was an interesting conversation. She said that she had spoke to investigators from the Nevada Financial Institution Division the same day she reported the letter, and then again, a few days later. Apparently, they came by her house when they spoke to her that second time. She said they asked if she had access to client accounts. As she explained to us, she informed them that she focused solely on administrative tasks such as scheduling appointments, drafting letters, filing paperwork and things along those lines."

"So what's her sense?" Bill asked, "does she believe that they suspect her of somehow being involved?"

"According to her, no. She says they didn't stay long, didn't have too many questions and they led her to believe that based on the evidence they had already recovered, they didn't suspect her of anything."

"Well that's good," said Mary.

"You and Vallory weren't there the other day ... "

"Where?" Sandra asked.

"Over at Bill and Chad's when we were putting the final touches on coordinating this little shindig. You and Val were over at Bruce Trent Park," continued George. "But anyway, Charles was telling us what he had read about BFSG and Morrison the other day. Did you guys read that piece in the *Las Vegas Business Press*?"

"Not I," said Vallory as Sandra shook her head, indicating that she also had not heard.

"Well, apparently - correct me if I'm wrong or miss anything, Charles - the Nevada Financial Institution Division had turned the case over to the Securities & Exchange Commission and they had filed suit alleging that Morrison and BFSG committed fraud by misappropriating and failing to segregate customer funds. The investigation, now being lead by the FBI, revealed that there has been a shortfall in customer funds dating back to at least June 2013."

"June of 2013? no shit?" asked Vallory.

"No shit. The BFSG funds that they have been able to track up to this point have been frozen and will be held in a trust pending the appointment of a trustee who will determine the structure of the payouts to former BFSG clients. Of course, at this point, no one knows where Morrison or the missing funds are. The only thing they do know, or at least are saying publicly at this point, is that they have some evidence suggesting that our boy, Carlton F. Morrison III, initially flew to Aruba."

"Shoot, we already knew that," said Sandra.

"Ah, true," Vallory said, "but they don't know that we already knew and that is the way it has to stay." Vallory started to make another comment, but changed her mind as the waiter approached their table.

"Good evening ladies and gentlemen. My name is Sean and I will have the pleasure of serving you this evening. To start you off, please enjoy the olives marinées and oefus mimosa and to Vallory and Sandra, que tous vos souhaits d'anniversaire se réalisent."

"Well okay, thank you, Sean," said Vallory. As Sean departed, Vallory and Sandra simply turned to Bill.

"May your birthday wishes come true. I'm sorry, it's 'may all your birthday wishes come true.'"

"Well, I have my health, my mental acuity is solid, I remain on financially solid ground and perhaps most importantly, I am blessed to be in the company of such good friends ... I would say my birthday wishes have already come true." Raising her glass, Sandra looked at Bill, "how do you say 'cheers' in French, my friend?"

"Try à votre santé."

"Alright then, to you my friends, I say, " à votre santé."

The meal was sublime and deep into the night they talked, laughed and danced. The Motor City Revue played all the right songs at all the right times. From Marvin Gaye to The Supremes and to Smoky Robinson from Motown, to Otis Redding and Booker T. & the MG's from the old Stax records label, the music was great. Vallory couldn't remember the last time she had such a good time.

EPILOGUE

Chicago. A fugitive and former resident of Las Vegas, Carlton F. Morrison III, has been apprehended by the Federal Bureau of Investigation at O'Hare International Airport while trying to sneak back into the United States. The founder and CEO of Blackstone Financial Services Group, 65, has been charged with financial fraud and malfeasance. The Securities & Exchange Commission filed suit last year, alleging that Mr. Morrison forged financial documents to steal more than $5.85 million from 28 clients, primarily retirees, over an 18 month period.

The investigation, led by the FBI's Las Vegas Division, revealed a shortfall in customer funds dating back to at least June 2013. Funds from the Blackstone Financial Services Group that have been recovered, $2.4 million at this point, have been placed under the care of Mr. Marvin J. Falcone, a court-appointed trustee. Mr. Falcone will determine the structure and amount payable to affected former BFSG clients.

In addition to the criminal case being brought in Federal court by the SEC, Morrison has been named as the defendant in a civil lawsuit brought by the plaintiffs, a small group of former BFSG clients. Details of that suit are not known at this time.

Speaking on condition of anonymity, an FBI official said Tuesday that Morrison had been attempting to travel to Pennsylvania to visit his ailing 92-year old mother. Authorities were alerted to his possible attempt at re-entry by his son, Mr. Jeremiah Morrison of Texas. Mr. John J. Walston, the attorney for the younger Mr. Morrison, has indicated his client does not have any comments at this time.

Carlton F. Morrison III is currently being transported back to Nevada where he is expected to appear at the United States District Court - Court of Nevada, on Thursday.

WORKS CONSULTED

Certified Financial Planner Board of Standards, Inc. *Financial Self-Defense Guide for Seniors: Know the red flags and avoid financial abuse.* 2012

Internal Revenue Service. *Tax Rules on Early Withdrawals from Retirement Plans.* November 2013

U.S. Securities and Exchange Commission. *Investor Bulletin: Accredited Investors.* September 2013

ABOUT THE AUTHOR

James C. Molet is the author of *Cream City Hustle* and *RENDEZVOUS WITH RETIREMENT: A Guide to Getting Fiscally Fit.* He retired from the United States Army in 2005 following 21 years of service. He holds an MBA from Wayland Baptist University. He lives in Arizona with his wife and can be reached via his website, http://RetirementSavvy.net.

43168400R00105

Made in the USA
San Bernardino, CA
15 December 2016